More praise for
Where Winners Live

"*Where Winners* live takes a no-victims approach to a highly demanding industry that positions individuals to take the driver's seat to their success. It is chock-full of relevant examples and anecdotes that not only support the novice, but can also advance the seasoned sales professional. This should be required reading for everyone in or entering the sales profession."

—**Karen Agrait**, CEO and president,
E-daptive Training Solutions

"*Where Winners Live* helped me realize that I have complete control over my successes as well as my failures. As a new financial advisor, this book has encouraged me to look at my business from a different perspective, and I am now on the right track. It has been enlightening to be 100 percent personally accountable for my life, both professionally and personally."

—**Kathleen Barlow**, financial advisor, Edward Jones

"Reading *Where Winners Live* is like being mentoring by people who have become successful and are willing to tell you how they got there. If you want to be successful selling high-value services, *Where Winners Live* is an important read."

—**Robert Friedman**, president, Fearless Branding

"True to Linda Galindo's trademark sassy and staccato style, *Where Winners Live* delivers 'lessons learned' from Dave Porter, punctuated with Linda's tough-love talk about clear agreements, responsibility, self-empowerment, and accountability. This is useful content for any selling, financial services, or client service professional. A great read!"

—**Todd Herman**, founder, Todd Herman Associates

"Even if you think of yourself as an accountable person, *Where Winners Live* helps you solidify how you act and how you live when you are 100 percent accountable to yourself. This common sense approach to accountability is useful to anyone who is trying to figure out, 'Why me?' and for those who think, 'Why *not* me?' It's the new management book for winners."

—**Dr. Cynthia McGovern**, founder and
First Lady of Sales, Orange Leaf Consulting

JB JOSSEY-BASS™
A Wiley Brand

Where Winners Live

Sell More, Earn More, Achieve More Through Personal Accountability

Dave Porter and Linda Galindo
with Sharon O'Malley

WILEY

Cover design by Adrian Morgan
Cover image : © Thinkstock

Published by Jossey-Bass
A Wiley Imprint
One Montgomery Street, Suite 1200, San Francisco, CA 94104-4594—www.josseybass.com

Jossey-Bass books and products are available through most bookstores. To contact Jossey-Bass directly call our Customer Care Department within the U.S. at 800-956-7739, outside the U.S. at 317-572-3986, or fax 317-572-4002.

Wiley publishes in a variety of print and electronic formats and by print-on-demand. Some material included with standard print versions of this book may not be included in e-books or in print-on-demand. If this book refers to media such as a CD or DVD that is not included in the version you purchased, you may download this material at http://booksupport.wiley.com. For more information about Wiley products, visit www.wiley.com.

Library of Congress Cataloging-in-Publication Data

Porter, Dave, 1961-
    Where winners live : sell more, earn more, achieve more through personal accountability / Dave Porter and Linda Galindo with Sharon O'Malley. — First edition.
        pages cm
    Includes index.
    ISBN 978-1-118-43626-4 (cloth), ISBN 978-1-118-46135-8 (ebk.),
    ISBN 978-1-118-46137-2 (ebk.), ISBN 978-1-118-46138-9 (ebk.)
        1. Selling. 2. Responsibility. 3. Success in business. 4. Career development.
    5. Business ethics. I. Galindo, Linda A. II. O'Malley, Sharon. III. Title.
    HF5438.25.P675 2013
    650.1—dc23
                                                                            2012042171

Printed in the United States of America
FIRST EDITION
HB Printing   10 9 8 7 6 5 4 3 2 1

Contents

DAVE PORTER
For Tom Quirk, my friend and mentor.
You took a young man without a sense for business and made a
businessman out of him.

LINDA GALINDO
For Grace
"When the student is ready, the teacher will appear."
—Buddhist proverb

Introduction

Mary started working as a financial planner and insurance sales-woman right after New Year's Day three years ago. By the end of her first year, the bright twenty-five-year-old had earned $60,000 in commissions. During Year Two, she took home $140,000. And this New Year's Eve, she and her new husband will join her company's CEO and her top-producing peers in Orlando for a four-day, all-expenses-paid conference that includes plenty of time to enjoy the theme parks, soak up the sunshine, and revel in the $190,000 paycheck she has earned after just three years in a job she started with absolutely no experience in sales.

Her goal for Year Four: $250,000. Her chances of succeeding: enormous. Her strategy: self-motivation, hard work, and personal accountability.

Mary's cubicle-mate—at least that's what he was before she earned her way into a private office—won't be joining her in Orlando.

Hired two months before Mary, John, also twenty-five when he joined the midsize financial services firm, also earned around $60,000 in commissions during his first year on the job. He took home just about $62,000 in Year Two. And this year, he's hoping to at least match last year's earnings.

He knows he's not earning as much as his colleague or selling as much as the CEO expects of a third-year associate. But he has a good excuse: He broke his ankle playing basketball last year, and he had a hard time getting around on it for a couple of months. Plus, he lives a good distance from the office and it's not really worth it to try to get in early, because the commute is a bear during the morning rush hour.

Not only that, the CEO likes Mary better, so he gives her more referrals than he offers John. Oh, and a guy who owns a group of rotisserie chicken franchises led him on for months before throwing him over for a more experienced advisor at a competing firm, so the effort John spent cultivating that prospect turned out to be a big waste of time.

John's goal for Year Four: to keep his job. His chances of succeeding: slim. His strategy: excuses and finger-pointing.

Both colleagues are personable, outgoing, and have a knack for sales. Both impressed recruiters during their job interviews with their confidence and their plans for success. Both participated in company-sponsored orientations and training, spent time with an experienced mentor, and had access to the CEO and other executives when they needed advice, a pep talk, or a push in the right direction.

In fact, the two are friends. Yet one is on her way to the top and the other is about to be unemployed. The main difference between them? Mindset.

Mary has a mindset of 100 percent personal accountability. She believes that she is responsible for her own success and that nobody else can or will make her rich. She takes the risks and actions she believes are necessary to move her toward her goal to live in an upscale neighborhood, travel often, and want for nothing. In the office by 8 A.M. every day, she is constantly on the phone, cold-calling prospective clients, setting appointments, and closing deals.

At the end of every day, of every quarter, and of every year, she reviews her successes and failures and knows she alone is accountable for the choices she made and the actions she took. And she believes she alone is accountable for the consequences and outcomes of those choices—even on the rare occasions when the result is disappointing or even disastrous.

John has a different mindset. A clever guy and the life of every party, John has nearly 1,000 Facebook friends and gets more invitations to parties, dinners, and weekends with family, pals, and co-workers than he can accept. He was president of his senior class in college, won a seat on his small county's Republican Central Committee at age twenty-one, and believes he can talk anybody into anything.

During his first year as a financial planner, in fact, more than 80 percent of his commissions came from friends who bought from him. It didn't occur to him until well into Year Two on the job that the business opportunities among his limited pool of gainfully employed buddies eventually would taper off, leaving him no opportunity but to create clients out of strangers instead of making his fortune by selling only to friends.

When he reviews his day, his quarter, and his year, he chalks up his poor performance to rotten luck. He knows it's not his fault that more of his friends don't need life insurance policies or can't afford to invest in retirement savings accounts. Sure, he knows he is responsible for making a living, but hey, what's he supposed to do? Things just aren't going the way they should.

It might seem that John is not accountable, and that Mary is. The fact is, they both are accountable. They just live in different places.

Mary lives Where Winners Live. John lives on Planet What Should Be.

John is just as accountable for his lack of success as Mary is for her superstar status. John is accountable for his choice to start his work day after the rush hour subsides, and for his decision to ignore the advice of his mentors, who warned him against trying to build a career on the backs of his buddies instead of finding a more sustainable source of clients. Who else could be accountable for that?

He'll never admit it, of course. He might never even admit it to himself, because he doesn't have a mindset of accountability. He is accountable. But he doesn't believe he is.

If he did believe he was accountable, chances are good that he would be more successful. He would arrive at his desk earlier every day, even if that meant moving closer to the office. He would mine not only his network of personal acquaintances, but, like Mary, he would pull out prospecting lists and make call after call until enough potential new clients agreed to meetings that might turn into sales. He would take the risks and actions necessary to boost his income into a range that would assure him not only that he could keep his job, but that he could flourish in it. And he wouldn't spend a minute blaming circumstances beyond his control for his troubles.

Anyone who works in sales has met colleagues like John. Some have been in his shoes: blaming everybody but himself for his choices and mistakes.

The good news: A mindset of 100 percent personal accountability is just as available to John as it is to Mary. It is just as available to someone who is losing and wants to win as it is to someone who is already winning.

It's available to you. All you have to do is choose it.

A mindset of 100 percent accountability means you acknowledge, believe, and act on the fact that you, and you alone, are 100 percent responsible for your own successes, opportunities, and happiness. It means you blame nobody for anything. You point fingers at no one. You find no fault. You feel no guilt. You simply own your choices and every outcome of those choices—good and bad.

Embrace a mindset of 100 percent personal accountability and you will:

- Sell more and earn more money.
- Save time and alleviate stress.
- Increase client retention and satisfaction.
- Work better with colleagues and bosses.
- Be more satisfied with your job and with your own performance.

- Achieve even your highest reaching goals.
- Live Where Winners Live.

Personal accountability is the secret weapon of every successful sales professional.

It is the secret weapon of *Where Winners Live* co-author Linda Galindo, who transformed herself from the self-proclaimed Queen of Victims into an entrepreneur, business coach, consultant, and speaker whose typical audience numbers 500 or more.

It is the secret weapon of *Where Winners Live* co-author Dave Porter, who became the owner and CEO of Baystate Financial Services at age thirty-five and grew it into a $100 million-a-year business over the next fifteen years.

It is the secret weapon of your co-worker who sells enough to qualify for the exotic company-sponsored trips every year, and of the financial advisor at your firm whose lakefront vacation home you envy every time he shows off photos of his family's summer holidays.

Where Winners Live will show you that it is the secret weapon of successful people at every level, from newcomers to the sales field, to rising young stars, to high-earning professionals, to aspiring leaders, to CEOs.

Take a poll of your closest colleagues. Ask the following:

How much of your success is up to you, and how much of it is determined by other people, luck, and circumstances that seem beyond your control?

And answer the question yourself.

Think about whether the flat tire that made you late for a closing is responsible for the loss of the sale or if your boss's infatuation with a young colleague is responsible for your lack of referrals. Consider whether the rainstorm that postponed your golf game with a wealthy contractor killed the momentum that might have turned him from prospect to client. Or if your office-mate really stole an account out from under you when she was the first to call someone you had been meaning to contact.

Are you responsible for any of this? For some of it? How about for all of it?

How did your colleagues answer the question you asked them? A good bet: The more money they make, the more responsibility they acknowledge for every success and failure they touch, and the more personally accountable they are.

Adopt a mindset of 100 percent responsibility for everything you do—before you know how it's all going to work out—and chances are good that it will work out in your favor. That's because you will take the risks and actions you know are necessary to make sure it does. Then, after all is said and done, stand up and own the result and the consequences of those risks and actions. Own the outcome—even if it's not the one you had hoped for. Even if it embarrasses you. Even if it will get you into trouble with your boss.

Stand up and be accountable.

Own every lost sale, every missed opportunity, every prospect who said "no." Identify what went wrong and how you contributed to the unwanted outcome. Determine what you could have done to get the result you wanted.

Own those missteps with as much gusto as you claim your most awesome successes. They're equally important to your future. And they're equally yours.

You are accountable. Admit it, accept it, acknowledge it, and embrace it. Learn from it. Act on it. Do better next time because of it.

Live Where Winners Live.

Whether you are just starting your career or have devoted your life to the sales profession, you can earn more, sell more, and achieve more through personal accountability.

Whether you are a rank-and-file employee or a corporate leader, you can improve your life and your fortunes through personal accountability.

This book will show you how.

Part I

ACCOUNTABILITY AND YOU

CHAPTER

1

YOU *ARE* ACCOUNTABLE

"It's a fact of life to be accountable."
—*Chris Litterio, managing partner*

You were born an accountable person. That you are accountable is as unchangeable as your height, the size of your feet, the color of your skin, and who your birth parents are. Some things just are what they are. Accountability is one of those things.

As surely as you breathe the air, you are accountable. Even if we claim we are not—and we claim it often—we are still accountable. We can say we refuse to be accountable, but we still are accountable. Others can claim we are not accountable, but we are accountable.

We don't take or choose accountability. We simply are accountable whether we like it or not, whether we want it or not.

Not everyone admits it, though. Not everyone even believes it. And not everyone has a mindset of accountability. If everyone on the planet did, the world would be home to fewer scandals, crises, wars, economic crashes, and crimes. If everyone at work did, the office would be a place of greater harmony, higher productivity, steeper profits, and happier associates.

If you believe you are accountable, you can enjoy a more successful career, more satisfying relationships, a lusher lifestyle, and a fatter paycheck—if those are things you want.

Samuel, a sales manager, says he wants those things, but he doesn't have them. He doesn't have the mindset. Samuel and his six-member team help field representatives assemble information before they go to meetings with clients. These sales professionals often need that information in a hurry.

Before he left the office on Monday night, Samuel scheduled a 9 A.M. conference call for the next day with a financial advisor who needed some last-minute help preparing for a 9:45 A.M. meeting. Early Tuesday morning, after a late night with some college buddies who were in town, Samuel called in sick. He told the colleague who answered his 8:15 A.M. call to notify the advisor that the conference call was off. The colleague forgot.

The advisor threw a fit when Samuel didn't call and didn't answer his phone. Samuel responded by blaming his absent-minded colleague. The colleague insisted it wasn't her responsibility to notify the advisor. Their manager chastised both, saying Samuel could have notified the advisor himself via e-mail and the co-worker who took the early morning call could have done the same.

Weeks later, Samuel still blames his colleague for what happened next: Because the advisor did not have the information he needed for his 9:45 A.M. meeting, he gave his client a price estimate that was too low. His choice: Take a huge hit on his commission or risk alienating the client by righting the price. He took the hit.

So did Samuel. The advisor complained about him to his boss and to his boss's boss, and the advisor will never trust his own sales manager again.

Another manager in the same company resolved another situation in a different way. At twenty-five, Tim is his firm's youngest manager, so he's diligent about building a reputation as a reliable professional whom financial advisors can count on—despite his inexperience.

So it cut him to the core when an advisor e-mailed him to say, "I guess you don't want to help me. I'll let everybody know." Tim didn't know what the advisor was talking about. He wanted to help. So he scoured prior e-mails in a hunt for the advisor's request. He couldn't find it. He asked a team member to take over another small case he had been working on, and he called the advisor immediately to tell him he had not seen the original request but would answer his questions right away.

That salvaged the relationship: "I followed through on the solution, and now, it's like it never happened," Tim says.

He also put a new process in place for his team. Tim has his team phone anyone who e-mails in a request to acknowledge the correspondence within minutes of receiving it. The team member estimates how long it will take to research and fill the request. That way, if the information doesn't come immediately, the caller will understand why. And the manager can determine how time-sensitive the request is.

Tim knows he is accountable for meeting the expectations of the sales professionals he supports. So he manages those expectations.

"We under-promise and over-deliver," he says. "When you're getting eight to twelve e-mails an hour, you can't get everything done right away. What you can do is call the advisor to work out a delivery time."

Tim has a mindset of accountability. He also has better relationships with the advisors than Samuel does; they trust him to follow-up with them to make sure their requests get filled. His days are far less stressful than Samuel's, and he can't remember the last time an advisor went over his head to complain about him to his boss.

Tim is what he was born to be: personally accountable for his choices and actions.

CHAPTER

2

WHAT IS ACCOUNTABILITY?

> "Do what you said. Finish what you start. Say please
> and thank you. Be on time."
>
> —*Dave Porter, CEO*

For Alan, an accredited estate planner and licensed financial planner, accountability is a rainbow. An engineer and frustrated painter, Alan's father encouraged his two sons to "bring the rainbow to everything; to bring the colors, because it makes a beautiful picture."

To the nine-year-old Alan, that meant any finished product "should shine like a rainbow, so somebody knows you were there." It meant knowing he did his best—and being honest about it if he didn't.

To the fifty-five-year-old Alan, who earned $1 million last year, it means looking every client in the eye and promising—with a clear conscience—that he did the best job he could do. And it means explaining exactly what that entailed, even if the outcome wasn't perfect. His measure of how well that works for him is the huge number of clients who personally recommend him to their friends, colleagues, and family members.

Alan lives Where Winners Live.

For Ann, accountability means keeping her promises. When Ann was six years old, her mother got a vacuum cleaner for Christmas. Little Ann was so enamored of that shiny, new machine that she promised her mother she would be in charge of vacuuming from then on. Mother was happy to indulge her little girl's pledge. In fact, she held Ann to that naive promise for twelve more years, and Ann was required to vacuum the house every week until she left for college.

"It wasn't an option not to do it," recalls Ann, now a chief operating officer. "We all had rules and chores within the family." She never skipped a week, so she was never punished for wiggling out of the chore. "There were never any threats. In our family, if you said you would do it, you did it because you made the commitment."

Forty years later, Ann runs her department the same way. "There's no threat at work," she says. "You need to follow through. You're expected to follow through. If you don't, I say, 'I thought we were clear on this. Let's get clear now.'"

Ann lives Where Winners Live.

Salesman-turned-CEO Dave's parents instilled in him a four-point definition of accountability:

- Do what you said.
- Finish what you start.
- Say please and thank you.
- Be on time.

Today, Dave runs a $100 million-plus company. He still follows these rules, and he expects his associates to respect them as well. Dave lives Where Winners Live.

Defining accountability will help you embrace a *mindset* of accountability. It will help you understand why being accountable is important to you, how it has helped you so far, and where it can lead you in the future.

Accountability has three facets:

- *Responsibility.* Be responsible for the success or failure of everything you do—for your choices, behaviors, and actions—*before* you know how it will all turn out. Own all of it, even if you're working for or with somebody else.
- *Self-empowerment.* Empower yourself to succeed. Take the actions—and the risks—that are needed to ensure that you achieve the results you desire.
- *Personal accountability.* Be accountable for your actions. Demonstrate your willingness to answer for the outcomes that result from your choices, behaviors, and actions, without fault, blame, or guilt—whether that outcome is good or bad.

What is your definition of accountability? Give it some thought.

Don't rely on or wait for your boss, colleagues, or clients to hold you accountable. Don't give away your power to define accountability for yourself, to be the architect of your own mind-set. Demonstrate your commitment to personal accountability so nobody needs to question whether you are accountable or tell you how to think or behave.

Do what you said. Finish what you start. Say please and thank you. Be on time.

Live Where Winners Live.

HOW ACCOUNTABLE ARE YOU?

1. I have a clear definition of what "accountability" means to me. Accountability is

   _____

   _____

   _____

2. Rate yourself on a 1 to 5 scale in the following areas. 1 = Poor, and 5 = Excellent

   _____ I do what I say I will do.

   _____ I finish what I start.

   _____ I say please and thank you.

   _____ I am on time.

3. Ask five colleagues to score you, and compare their scores to yours.

   _____

   _____

   _____

   _____

   _____

   Do you know yourself? Winners do.

CHAPTER

3

LINDA'S STORY

"I don't go a day without saying this out loud: 'I own this.'"

—*Linda Galindo, accountability thought leader, speaker, coach, consultant, author*

Linda is the first to admit she once claimed the title "Queen of Victims."

She's not ashamed of it, because that low point in her life eventually led her to develop a mindset of accountability with a huge payoff: She gets to work for herself, to help others achieve their goals, and to assist executives at the highest level as they create workplaces where accountability is embraced and expected.

She couldn't have done any of that twenty years ago, however. She could barely stand up straight after spending so much time and energy complaining, feeling sorry for herself, and blaming the world for her troubles.

She had good reason to be in a bad mood: She had a crummy job, a mean boss, pessimistic parents, and a bad marriage. She had nothing to be happy about or look forward to. No wonder she whined about it all the time. Even her best friends got tired of her constant complaining, and one by one, they stopped taking her calls. But one especially good friend stuck around, and that friend changed Linda's life.

This good friend asked Linda, "Have you ever considered that you might have something to do with the unhappy situation you find yourself in?" The truth is, Linda hadn't considered that she was responsible for her own bad mood, for choosing to stay in a demeaning job, for putting up with a marriage that no longer worked. She blamed all of that on other people and her upbringing. It couldn't be her fault.

She had the mindset of a victim. She didn't realize that blaming everyone and everything for her unhappiness would never cure her of it. She didn't realize that finding fault with others—or even with herself—would never make her happy.

So she toyed with changing her mind. She considered moving to Planet What Is, a place where she could accept her circumstances for what they were: *hers*. On Planet What Is, she could realize that her own choices and behaviors had created those circumstances. She could realize that she had chosen an unhappy life.

It sounds like a good move, but she didn't go to Planet What Is—at least not right away. Giving up a kingdom that had taken her a lifetime to build turned out to be too difficult. Giving up her crown and scepter would mean she had nobody but herself to blame for her hard times.

So she clung to her convictions: She was right; everyone else was to blame. That felt familiar and sort of comfortable. But being right didn't make her happier, didn't land her in a better job, and didn't make it any easier to live in an unhappy home. That's because blaming someone else for your problems doesn't solve them.

So when she got sick enough of living on Planet What Should Be, she packed her bags and moved. Literally. She got a divorce, found a new job, made peace with her parents, and admitted that wallowing in self-pity is a choice.

When her friends came back around, they were delighted that Linda's luck had changed. But it hadn't. What had changed was Linda's mindset.

With her new mindset of accountability, Linda realized she owned her choices and her actions, and she owned the results of those choices and actions. And if she owned the results, she had better make sure she did whatever it took to get good results.

Today, Linda's results are usually pretty great, as is true for most people with a mindset of accountability. As she starts any new day or project, she remembers that she is responsible for her actions and choices; now, she suffers fewer failures and enjoys more success.

Still, when things don't go as planned, she stands up and owns her failures. She learns from them, she corrects her mistakes, she grows as a result, and she moves on without pointing fingers or spending her energy feeling sorry for herself. And she doesn't go a day without saying out loud: *I own this*.

ARE YOU A VICTIM OR A WINNER?

Recall a recent situation at work that did not go as you planned or hoped it would. Suspend all blame and finger-pointing for purposes of this exercise. Assume you are the only one who owns the outcome of the situation.

1. Explain *why* you own the disagreement, misunderstanding, mistakes, or whatever happened to make this a stressful experience that turned out badly. Don't say, "I don't own any of this." Instead, go with, "I own all of it. Just me. It's mine."

2. Describe how you will use this mindset of personal ownership to influence the outcome the next time you face a similar situation.

CHAPTER

WHERE LOSERS LANGUISH

> "I look at myself in the mirror and I ask myself, 'Am
> I doing the best I can possibly do?' If the honest
> answer is 'no,' I hold myself accountable. Nobody
> has more of an interest in my success than I do."
>
> —*Kareen Blake, financial advisor*

Not everyone lives Where Winners Live—at least not yet. You might recognize your colleagues—or yourself—among those who are minus the mindset. Do you recognize yourself among the eleven types of behaviors discussed in this chapter? Would your colleagues say they recognize you?

Be honest. Then think about how you can change your behavior so it has no trace of these loser characteristics.

The Victim

You've already met one victim: Linda, before she adopted a mindset of accountability. Victims seem perpetually down on their luck with no hope of improving it.

Victims are guys like Mark, who just can't catch a break. He's a nice enough fellow, but you can't have a conversation with him that doesn't include a litany of wrongs that have befallen him, through no fault of his own—or at least that's how he tells it.

Mark didn't meet his sales quota last month because the realtor he was hoping to talk into handing over her client list got called away for a funeral. The month before that, he would have done OK, except his kid got sick while his wife was out of town. A flat tire ruined his whole week and a sore throat on Tuesday morning so severely slowed down his call schedule that he couldn't contact any prospects for days.

Mark will never get ahead, because he's blaming everyone and everything but himself for his poor performance. He hasn't figured out that he can work around life's inevitable blips, set contingency plans, and decide he will succeed with or without the help of any single person.

In Mark's world, circumstances beyond his control dictate his success. He has no power.

The Finger-Pointer

It's a joy to take credit for your decisions and actions when everything turns out well. It can be torture to admit you're responsible for those same choices when they result in catastrophe.

So the finger-pointer "owns" only the good.

We landed the client?

I had her eating out of my hand!

She signed with our competitor instead?

My assistant really messed this up when he called her by the wrong name.

The finger-pointer has this mindset: I'm accountable for my results when they are good; someone else is to blame for my results when they are bad.

But it's unlikely anybody but the finger-pointer believes that is true.

The Robbery Victim

This colleague is always telling people he's "been robbed."

> "Patty stole my client. I was planning to call him next week to get something started."

> "That was *my* trip. The only reason Andrea got the last seat at the conference is because I was on vacation last week."

> "I deserve credit for that sale. My manager swooped in just as I was on the verge of closing the deal and took it away from me, like he didn't trust me to get it done or something. That should have been *my* commission."

The robbery victim always blames someone else for undermining him, for getting something he deserved instead, or for scoring a win at her expense. He's the skinflint who can't open a pickle jar and then says of the muscle-bound guy who screws off the lid, "I loosened it for him."

The Coulda-Woulda

Susan could have had the promotion if she had wanted it. She would have been Salesperson of the Year if her coworker, James, hadn't lucked into that last-minute, half-million-dollar sale. She could have made that sale herself if the boss didn't always play favorites, which is how James got invited to the party where he met the wealthy client.

The coulda-woulda tries to take credit for what she didn't earn by saying she easily could have, if only . . . (take your pick of excuses). Often, she pretends she didn't want it, but she protests too loudly about the one who won for anybody to buy that act.

The Gossip

Perhaps the most vicious of all workplace losers, the gossip puts others down in an attempt to make himself seem better.

The strategy very rarely works, however; the gossip doesn't gain any credibility or respect by talking about others behind their backs or by spreading lies and rumors about people. What the gossip does—in a surprisingly effective way—is damage the reputations of those he whispers about.

Emily knows that all too well. She worked as the top assistant to Angela, a wildly successful advisor. After an uncomfortable telephone conversation with a long-time client of the insurance practice, Emily was visibly upset. Another assistant, Elliott, asked her what was wrong, and Emily told him the A-list client had made an outrageous accusation, saying that Angela sold him a high-dollar annuity that he did not need just because she would reap a hefty commission from the sale, and then she ignored him after the deal was final. Emily had assured the client that the advisor would never make a sale that wasn't in a customer's best interest and promised that Angela would call him as soon as she came back to the office for the afternoon.

Then Emily left for lunch. As soon as she did, Elliott started texting other assistants to tell them that this top-producing advisor, a favorite of the CEO's, had broken the rules of client suitability and angered an important client. One of those assistants works for the CEO, and she repeated the story to him.

The CEO, of course, takes accusations seriously, but not gossip. So he confronted Angela, satisfied himself the sale was on the up and up, and called the client personally to smooth his ruffled feathers.

Then Angela fired Emily for breaching the client's confidentiality and the advisor's trust. And Elliott still has his job.

The Should-er

If you're not careful, this one will "should" all over you.

You should call more prospects.

You should fire your assistant.

You should combine your practice with Joe's.

Maybe you should, and maybe you shouldn't. Whether you will is completely up to you. So why are so many people trying to decide for you?

Beware of the should-er. A couple of them almost had Lisa convinced to completely change her game—against her wishes.

For a dozen years, Lisa has endured the criticism of bosses and colleagues because she works only a few cases at a time and spends what they say is way too much time on each one. Yet she meets her personal income goals every year and qualifies to attend all of her firm's high-earner conferences.

Still, she took what others told her to heart and worked hard to expand her client list, with modest success. Then, she had an epiphany: She was an "elephant hunter."

She and some colleagues studied the practices of the ten top advisors at the financial services firm where they work to try to uncover the secrets of those superstars' success. What they learned was that all of the big guns took one of four paths:

- They created a niche business to serve an exclusive clientele, such as doctors.
- They partnered with another successful financial advisor.
- They shared clients with influential nonfinancial professionals, such as accountants and attorneys.
- They were "elephant hunters" who focused on only a few, very large clients and provided them with concierge-quality service.

Validated, Lisa stopped trying to change her practice to please critics whose goals were different from hers and who were "shoulding" all over her. Instead, she redoubled her focus on wealthy individuals and large corporations that brought her so much business that she didn't need a slew of them.

She's accountable for her limited client list and committed to the focus she has chosen. "It's time to admit this is what I'm doing, commit to it, and stop trying to do something else just because people say I should," she says.

The We-We

Hitch your boat to the we-we and you'll float right past your goals without having time to achieve any of them. The we-we has great ideas and usually agrees with yours when it comes to what "we" should do.

Dana, an average-earning insurance agent, convinced Carrie, a certified financial planner, to merge their practices so each one could service the other's clients. That appeared to Carrie to be a sound plan—until she realized Dana is a we-we.

"We should put together a kit for our clients with a letter explaining our partnership and brochures describing our combined products and services," Dana offered.

"I love that idea," Carrie responded. "I'd also like to plan an open house for our clients to come in and see our new office and hear about some new products."

Once it was clear the pair agreed on their new promotional plan, Carrie pulled up her daily planner and prepared to find time for her share of the tasks. "OK, let's work on the kit first," offered Carrie. "I'll write the text for the financial services part of the brochure, and you can take care of the insurance section. Can you write your section by next Friday?"

"I'm really not a good writer," Dana responded. "I don't think I'm the one for that job."

"OK," Carrie compromised, "I'll write the whole brochure then. Why don't you find a printing company to design the brochure and print it for us?"

"I don't know anything about printing companies," Dana countered. "It would be better if somebody else did that."

Carrie got the same story when she asked Dana to pitch in with the letter, the open-house invitations, the refreshments, and their presentation. Turns out when Dana said "we" should do it, she meant Carrie should do it.

A caution about the we-we: She will create a river of extra work for you. A "we" unowned, after all, is a job undone. And every accountable sales professional knows every "what" needs a "who" and a "by when."

The Yes Man

They say if you want something done, ask a busy person to do it. The yes man is a busy person, and he'll agree to do anything you ask him.

Trouble is, he's *too* busy, because he never says no. So there's no way he can do everything everybody asks him to do—at least not on time.

"Yes" is not an honest word when the person who says it is agreeing to something he knows he can't do by the promised deadline.

Yes man Paul was so overbooked with client appointments one week last month that he chose to cancel a weekend getaway with his family so he could work on Saturday and Sunday to catch up on paperwork and follow up with the clients he met during the week. Yet when his colleague, Martha, poked her head into his office on Thursday evening and asked Paul to cover for her with her clients while she enjoyed a long weekend away, he agreed.

As he tiptoed out of the house at 6 A.M. on Saturday, trying his best not wake his already-disappointed wife, his mobile phone rang. It was a client of Martha's with an emergency that needed immediate attention. So Paul postponed his trip to the office and drove fifty miles to the client's house—and spent most of the day there helping Martha's client.

He worked on paperwork all day Sunday, but he never got around to following up with his own clients, and he started the week on Monday about eight hours in the hole when it came to his schedule.

Now his clients were as annoyed as his family. So why didn't he just tell Martha he was too busy to cover for her?

Everybody likes Paul, and he likes it that they do. Saying no, he fears, would change his colleagues' opinion of him as a guy who would do anything for anybody.

Yet saying yes is not accountable. Paul can't possibly do what he said he would do, finish what he started, or get everything done on time if he doesn't limit his to-do list to the number of hours in his work week—or in this case, in his botched weekend.

"No" is an empowering word. It's an honest word. It will keep you accountable.

The Guess Man

Hard as you try, you will never quite figure out what the guess man expects you to do.

The guess man could be a colleague or a boss. He's the guy who assigns you a project but is not clear about the result he expects. Or he's a teammate who takes on a task he doesn't understand, but doesn't ask any questions to clarify his role or his goal.

There can be no accountability without clarity, and the guess man knows this. The more vague he is with his instructions, the easier it will be to blame someone else when the job doesn't go well.

Glenn runs a small insurance practice about twenty-five miles away from the city. He employs two young sales professionals and an assistant who helps all three.

His younger colleagues have a few of their own clients, but for most, the three professionals share the job of contacting prospects, following up with them, and doing research and paperwork. Still, Glenn likes to be the "face" of the practice, so he handles most of the in-person client meetings.

Everyone in the practice was delighted when the parents of a long-time client decided to bring their business to Glenn. The team prepared to get busy reviewing the couple's existing policies, advising them about how to make the switch from their former insurance firm, whose principal had retired, and preparing their applications to send to the underwriters.

Glenn called an impromptu meeting of his staff to divvy up the tasks quickly. He assigned Wanda to compile information about the couple's existing policies and asked Jay to do some research on additional products that might benefit the family. He put Kara, the assistant, on alert to help as needed, and said he would meet with the clients personally to present the information. Then he called the couple and scheduled an appointment for 11 A.M. Friday.

At 3 P.M. Thursday, he started to prepare for his meeting. He asked Kara to bring him all of the information submitted by Wanda and Jay. She didn't have it.

Wanda had taken a few personal days and wouldn't be back until Monday. And Jay was waiting for Wanda to tell him about the couple's existing policies before he could suggest additional products.

Glenn was angry. "This always happens!" he fussed. "Why can't they just do what I need when I need it?" The answer to that question is pretty easy: He never told anyone when he needed it.

He canceled his Friday meeting. And on Monday, he berated his staff for his having to cancel the meeting and inconvenience the clients. In response, they blamed him for neglecting to give them a deadline.

The fact is, every person involved in the transaction—except for the clients—failed to be clear or get clear about their expectations. Glenn didn't assign a deadline. Wanda and Jay didn't ask when the work was due. And now they all had someone to blame if the client is disappointed or cancels the sale.

For the guess man, sometimes blame is more important than the sale itself.

The Sneak

To some, being accountable means being *held* accountable. The sneak, for example, believes she is accountable only if she gets caught.

The sneak takes her cues from the likes of the politicians and corporate leaders who wind up in the news because they choose to behave poorly and then deny, deny, deny, even after it is clear to everyone that they are guilty of the wrongdoing.

The sneak realizes that being accountable can have negative consequences, and she doesn't want to suffer the penalties for unethical, illegal, or just plain sneaky behavior.

The sneak says she doesn't know what she did was wrong. Or she says she didn't do what she's accused of doing, even when the evidence says she did.

The irony of that attitude is that the consequences of accountability often are less egregious than the fallout from denying your accountability.

You can pretend you're not accountable for your actions, but, truth is, you are accountable. If you deny your responsibility for your own choices and behavior, everyone will acknowledge your accountability but you. The sneak thinks she is getting away with something, but she's just not sneaky enough to fool anyone.

The Not-Good-Enougher

Few colleagues frustrate a highly accountable professional more than the not-good-enougher, who refuses to acknowledge a job well done. The not-good-enougher might be a teammate, a boss, or even a client who makes it clear that no matter what you do or how well you do it, it won't measure up, because the not-good-enougher is never satisfied.

When Phil hires new financial planners, he makes his expectations clear: They must contact enough prospects every day to land at least one new client a week. So during her first six months on the job, Kim made call after cold call, networked with her vast array of social media contacts, logged twelve-hour days, and consistently brought a new client a week into the firm.

Phil's response: Not good enough. Kim's impressive effort, he said, should reap a greater number of clients. And he kicked up her quota to three a week.

Exhausted, Kim chose not to put in additional hours or cram more cold calls into each already-packed day. In fact, she gave herself permission to shorten her work days, figuring if Phil upped her quota based on her hard work, she would work a little less hard.

Phil didn't expect his demand would lead Kim to slack off; he hoped it would propel her to greater productivity. But she realized that working harder and producing more would not be good enough for Phil—so why do it?

CHAPTER 5

WHERE DO YOU LIVE?

"Accountability is a holistic thing. It's not about making one good decision. It starts when the alarm clock goes off. Am I going to hit the snooze, or am I going to get out of bed?"

—*Bryan Morrell, team leader*

The eleven behavior types discussed in Chapter Four don't live Where Winners Live. Some live on Planet What Should Be. Others congregate in a mythical land where lies magically become the truth if you say them out loud and convince enough people to believe them. A few have set up residence in a neighborhood where failing with a good excuse means they're winners after all— at least in their own minds.

That's not Where Winners Live, however. Winners live on Planet What Is.

Shelley doesn't live anywhere near there. At twenty-seven, she just started her first full-time job.

She is humiliated every time she walks into the financial services firm where she works and takes her seat in her assigned cubicle, three-deep away from the window. She nearly cries every time she cashes her paycheck, because it barely covers the rent on her tiny apartment and the payments on her car and student loans.

She should be a big-shot on Wall Street by now. All of her college friends are already making six figures in similar jobs, and she should be, too. She should have finished graduate school three years ago instead of last year. It wasn't her fault that she had to sit out a semester and repeat so many classes; her history degree didn't prepare her for business school. Her parents shouldn't have pushed her into history. And it shouldn't have taken her a year after graduation to finally land a job.

Now she's three years behind her peers instead of sitting in the corner office where she belongs. She shouldn't have to "pay her dues," as everyone says. She shouldn't have to spend ten hours a day in the office making cold calls to faceless prospects. She shouldn't have to work so hard just to pay her rent. She should be lunching with wealthy clients and vacationing with top-performing colleagues on the company's dime.

Shelley knows she is not living the life she should be living.

Her biggest problem: She's living it on Planet What Should Be. She probably would earn more and move into that private office quicker if she based her choices and actions on *what is* rather than on what *should be*.

Shelley spends more time blaming her parents and her professors and her successful friends for her troubles than she does calling prospects. Chances are good that she will live in this mess she has made for a long, long time.

Where do you live? Do you live in a world where you can change your past by saying it should have been different? That's not going to happen. So you might as well pack up your woes and move to Planet What Is.

All that matters is what *is*. There you will find the way things *are*, not the way they should be.

Once you accept what *is*, you can figure out which risks and actions are necessary to get you what you would like to have, to earn the commissions you would like to earn, to take the trips you would like to take.

Staying angry at the past won't earn you that future. Blaming your parents, your teachers, your boss, or your spouse won't make that future happen for you.

Today simply is what it *is*. Deal with what *is* and you can change what will be. You'll never be able to change the past. Live in the past, and you'll continue to "should" all over yourself. Live on Planet What Is, and today will be more fulfilling than yesterday.

Moving to Planet What Is takes skill and courage. And it's time to make your move. There's plenty of room for you Where Winners Live.

CHAPTER

CHOOSING YOUR MINDSET

"Be true to yourself. Be true to your values. Be true
to what you believe in. Then, measure your results."
—*Greg Pinto, chief investment officer*

With three children—including one with special needs—and a wife waiting for him in the evening, Vince has to hurry home after work to be with his family. Yet to meet his financial goals, he must work many hours in his job as a financial planner.

He has figured out how to meet both obligations without working more than forty hours a week, however. His secret: He works hard every hour of those forty hours.

"As life goes on and you figure out what's really important, which is family, you realize you're going to work only so many hours," he says. "So I need to get as much as I can out of those hours."

To that end, Vince enlisted a time-management expert to help him stop wasting time. Now he turns off the car radio while driving home from work and powers up his Bluetooth so he can make hands-free business calls or dictate notes from the day's meetings into a service that transcribes his words and then e-mails them to his assistant. He uses an online calendar that reminds him of appointments and tasks.

Since he started using technology to help him manage his time, he rarely works past 6 P.M., and he earns 300 percent more in revenue than he did before he used these tactics.

"It took me a long time to understand that in an entrepreneurial model, the only limit you have on your income is yourself," says Vince, who has worked as a financial planner for fourteen years. "Then I realized I could make three times as much money if I worked harder and smarter."

Vince doesn't spend even one minute a day wishing his home life weren't so demanding or using it as an excuse to slack off on his work. If he did, his colleagues and even his boss probably would understand. But to Vince, that would waste time that he could spend making money. And he wants to make a lot of money.

He is accountable for how much money he makes. He is accountable for how he spends his time. He is accountable for being a dad who wants and needs to be home every night for dinner with his family.

Vince lives Where Winners Live: in a mindset of 100 percent accountability.

Katherine, however, doesn't live there.

She does well at work, but she doesn't earn 300 percent more than she did a few years ago, as Vince does. Still, she knows she is accountable for her success—mostly.

Occasionally, Katherine reasons, circumstances beyond her control cause her bad results. Take the weather, traffic, the occasional flat tire, or a restless night that left her without enough energy for her day.

So when she has an off day, or even an off quarter, she finds plenty of circumstances beyond her control to blame: her son's demanding soccer schedule, her mother-in-law's unexpected visit, a computer that crashed, Christmas preparations.

In fact, Katherine figures that at least 15 percent of the time, she really has no control over what happens during her day or how that day will turn out. She figures she is 85 percent responsible for the success of any given day, project, or goal, and circumstances beyond her control determine 15 percent of those outcomes.

She is accountable, with a caveat: She is not accountable for circumstances she considers beyond her control.

Back to Vince. It rains on his way to work as often as it does during Katherine's commute. But he leaves his house so early in the morning that he has plenty of leeway to deal with weather-delayed slow traffic and still arrive at work on time. He experiences few flat tires and car troubles because he knows a few minutes of preventive maintenance now will save him from losing up to an hour later if he has to change a flat or deal with a car issue on his way to work. He plows though the days when he feels sluggish or has the sniffles, because he knows each day will end at 6 P.M. and he needs to finish his work by then.

Vince chooses to be in charge of his day, choosing a mindset of 100 percent accountability. He chooses to have a successful day every day, no matter what circumstances beyond his control throw at him. Instead of blaming them, he figures out how to get around them. It's a great attitude, and it is available to everyone.

Few people live with a mindset of 100 percent accountability. It takes discipline and sacrifice. But, frankly, 85 percent accountability isn't a bad place to live.

In fact, if you believe that you are at least 85 percent responsible for your success—and that just 15 percent of the success of a project or a day or even your career could depend on chance or luck or your boss's mood—you'll get good results.

The accountability mindset can be measured on a scale that ranges from 0 to 100 percent. The higher the percentage of ownership you believe you have when you begin your day, a project, or your job, the more success you'll experience. *You* determine your level of achievement in advance.

Suppose, for example, that you have a client meeting at 2 P.M. today, and an edict came down yesterday requiring all

sales staff to offer a complicated new product to qualified customers. You could decide, "There's no way I can learn enough
about this new product by 2 P.M. to sell it to the client I'm
meeting. I've never worked with anything like this before, and
the company just dumped this on everyone at the last minute.
How can the boss expect me to sell something with so little
time to prepare? I'm not going to mention it to my client, and
then I guess I'll face the music when I report what happened."

Or you could tell yourself, "I'm sure I can persuade Joyce to
join my meeting. She's the one who's training everyone about
the new product, so she can explain all of its ins and outs to
my client. And if she can't travel to my client's office today, I'll
arrange to get her on Skype during the meeting."

You can decide to be a victim of your circumstances, or you
can outsmart them by taking the action necessary to get what
you need or want. You can decide whether outside conditions—
your lack of time, the short notice of the edict—will ruin your
meeting. Or you can decide not to let them. It's your choice.
Mindset is a choice. Letting outside conditions ruin your plans
is a choice. Overcoming obstacles is a choice.

Every morning, choose to own your day. Decide you will be
at least 85 percent responsible for every success and failure during that day—before you even know how it's going to turn out.
You'll work smarter if you know at the outset that you—and you
alone—are accountable at the end of the day for whether
you had a good day or a bad one.

Have a good day. Have an accountable day.

CHAPTER

7

CLARITY: THE CORE OF ACCOUNTABILITY

> "Personal accountability means if we have
> a discussion and we agree we're going to do
> something, that's what's going to be done. It's not
> a variation of what's going to be done. It's what's
> going to be done."
>
> —*Alan Bolotin, accredited estate planner,*
> *licensed financial planner*

Before a financial advisor meets with a new client for the first time, Caitlin, a financial planning director, typically sits down with the advisor to go over the products and plans that will drive the discussion during the meeting. She answers all of the advisor's questions and doesn't end the meeting until she is satisfied the advisor can comfortably explain the plan to the client.

Sometimes, the advisor asks Caitlin to join the meeting in case anything unexpected comes up. That's what happened during one recent client meeting. But the one caught off guard was Caitlin.

Once the advisor, the client, and Caitlin had shaken hands and comfortably settled into their chairs, the advisor asked Caitlin to run the meeting. Put on the spot, she did her best. She explained the plans and products, the firm's process, and the kind of relationship the client could expect to have with the advisor. But when it came time to quote the fee, Caitlin was unprepared. So she revealed the range of fees an advisor might collect.

After the meeting, the advisor told Caitlin he expected her to quote the client an exact fee—and that the fee would be on the high end of the scale she had outlined for the client during the meeting.

Caitlin chose not to blame the advisor for blindsiding her by asking her to take over a meeting that she hadn't prepared to run. But the advisor blamed her for undercutting his fee.

Caitlin took the miscommunication as a learning opportunity, and she immediately changed the way she preps advisors for first meetings with clients. Her first question for every advisor now: "What do you expect me to say during the meeting?" She digs deep into the nitty-gritty details so she can prepare an answer to any potential question from the client.

She created an assignment grid for each first client meeting. The grid indicates each discussion point or action that will come up during the meeting—from the opening remarks, to the introductions, to the explanation of products, to the quoting of fees. And next to each item, as the advisor looks on, she writes the name of the person who will handle that part of the meeting—either her name or the advisor's name.

"This way, there's never a situation where we are caught off guard," she says. "I never want to put the advisor—who's sitting in front of a client—off guard. It doesn't make them look good. They can always blame me later, but that doesn't salvage their relationship with the client."

Instead of blaming or chastising the advisor who put her on the spot, Caitlin directed her energy toward making sure it never happens again.

That's Where Winners Live. Winners live in a world of absolute clarity.

Caitlin's new practice is a smart one: She creates a perfectly clear agreement with the advisor about who will speak about what at a new-client meeting. The smartest part: She puts the agreement in writing.

Accountable people make clear agreements. The most effective agreement is written. The written agreement specifies who will do what, and by when. As with a contract, everyone involved signs the written agreement and agrees to comply. Everybody gets a copy; everybody buys in, and that buy-in makes it far more likely that everyone will honor the agreement.

People can be unclear about their expectations and commitments until they're tasked with writing them down. With a written agreement, everybody is accountable for exactly what he or she agrees to do, and each agrees to be accountable and meet the deadlines. With a written agreement, all involved can hold themselves and everyone else accountable for living up to that agreement. If a dispute or an objection arises later, the team can refer to the written agreement. It's a far more effective tool than a conversation with no written record of the promises made.

The effective written agreement covers the following:

- What is the task or project I am taking ownership of?
- What is the expected outcome or deliverable?
- What actions will I take to complete the task?
- What is the deadline for each task I have agreed to perform?
- What are the benefits of completing the tasks, and what are the consequences of not honoring the agreement?

In addition to making assignments perfectly clear, the written agreement can help keep you and your partners on track. It can help you schedule the work so you'll have time to complete it. It also can serve as a red flag if you realize, once you plug the work into your schedule, that you have inadvertently agreed to something you can't possibly accomplish by the deadline you agreed to.

Your teammates will appreciate you more if you contact them well in advance of the deadline to renegotiate that date instead of letting the due date slip away without giving anybody a heads-up that you won't be able to meet it.

In fact, when winners realize they can't meet their deadlines, they renegotiate them—well in advance—and never blow them off.

Working with others—with even one other person—requires some trust between partners. Your part of the project mostly likely will affect my part. I might not be able to finish or even start the tasks I have agreed to until you complete yours, or vice versa.

If your agreement is with a customer and you break it—even with a slight misstep, such as not following up until the day after you agreed to call—you can not only damage your relationship with the client, but you risk losing the sale and even souring the buyer against the company you work for or the brand of product you sell.

The people we trust are the people we can count on. Clarity and transparency build trust. If you want to know a project status, and someone is vague with the details or avoids answering your question, it's likely you will not trust that person. If you're the one who's being cagey, count on this: People will not trust you.

You can tell someone, "Trust me. I've got it covered. I'm on it." But in this fast-paced world of contracts and agreements for all things big and small, blind trust isn't the norm. And it's rarely a good choice.

You have to rely on *yourself* to be clear about the things that affect you. Often, that means slowing down and gauging how trustworthy the person or organization you're dealing with really is. Just as your trust is something you're slow to give away to others, those who deal with you are gauging whether they can give theirs to you. Build trust by being clear with others about what you will do and what you expect them to do. Build trust by clarifying with others what they will do and what they expect you to do. Then do what you said you would do. And hold them accountable for doing what they said they would do.

Broken agreements, ranging from showing up late for a meeting to failing to follow-up with someone by the appointed time, create distrust. If you consistently breach even the smallest agreements—the ones that seem to matter little to you—you build a reputation, a personal culture, of distrust.

You can build a personal culture of trust by taking care to honor the agreements you've made. Be accountable for those agreements. Be clear and transparent. Once you start, it becomes an unstoppable force. Until you do that, you will never be successful at holding others accountable. If it's OK for you to break an agreement, those whose feet you're holding to the fire will, very reasonably, figure that it's OK for them, too.

That will hurt you when you're leading a team, rising through the ranks in your organization, or building a business. It will hurt you when you're selling your company's products and services to skeptical clients.

Any lack of trust that surrounds you starts with you. Can you be trusted? Do you do what you say you will do, by when you agree to do it? Are you willing to make clear agreements? In writing? Yes, that pins you down, and that can seem uncomfortable and inflexible. But if you want to be trusted, that's the price you have to pay.

Would you like to have clarity, transparency, accountability, and the trust of those you work with and for? Or is it more important to retain some flexibility and wiggle room, and an environment where you can get away with excuses and justification?

Stop talking about how others can't be trusted. Instead, demonstrate, at every opportunity, that *you* can be trusted. Trust will not be legislated into existence. It's up to you to create it for yourself. To see it, you have to be it.

And that comes with some risk. A clearly written agreement will prevent you from claiming, if you don't do what you promised, that you didn't understand what you were supposed to do. It will shoot holes in just about any excuse you can come up with for not honoring the bargain you made. It will rob you of scapegoats. It will prevent you from playing the victim card.

Make clear agreements a routine practice whenever any other person—a boss, a colleague, or a client—is involved in any transaction with you. Clarity has two sides: being clear about what is expected of you, and making your expectations clear to others.

At his insurance firm, Alan learned a valuable lesson about expectations after he spent hours with a woman who cold-called his shop to ask for a quote for long-term care insurance. He educated her about his services and explained that long-term care insurance might not be the right product for her. He did some research on her behalf and offered her several alternative products that would be more suitable, given her circumstances.

She wound up buying long-term care insurance from another provider at a different company—because she wanted that product and she wanted it for the cheapest price. Now, Alan treats potential new clients a little differently. Now he expects—and gets—them to be absolutely clear with him about what they want from him from the get-go. He came up with a checklist to make his client conversations more fruitful.

Here is Alan's checklist for his initial conversation with a potential client:

❑ Is this client a "fit" for our practice? Is she looking for someone to help her plan her future and manage her money?
   Or does she believe insurance is a commodity and that it doesn't matter from whom she buys it?
❑ Can she articulate what she's looking for in a financial planner?
❑ Is she willing to talk about what she needs in terms of products and services, or does she trust the advice of friends and celebrities more than a licensed financial planner?
❑ Will she be honest about her financial situation: where she is, where she has been, and where she wants to go financially?

This is especially important for would-be clients who have had a bad experience with prior investments and might be reluctant to trust a product, or even a planner, again.

❏ What does she expect me to be for her? A planning partner? An advisor? A decision-maker? An order-taker? A magician?

❏ Is she looking for a long-term relationship?

❏ Will she make a commitment to work only with me?

❏ If not, will she pay a fee for my time?

Once you make your expectations clear, you are halfway toward achieving the clarity you need to move forward with any project, sale, or agreement. Then you need to get clear about the expectations of everyone else involved in the transaction.

You can do the time-consuming dance with people who are "shopping around" for the best quotes but really don't care whom they dance with. Or you can get clear from the start about what callers want, so you can decide if you want to spend your time that way.

And it doesn't end once you land a client or close a sale. Alan, for one, doesn't stop asking his clients questions, even after he has established trusting, years-long relationships with them. He figures his clients stay with him for so long because they trust him, and he continually gauges just how much.

Make it a practice to ask your clients routinely if you are meeting their expectations. Even if they say yes, ask them what they expect. Being clear means making your expectations clear to clients, staff, bosses, and anyone you work with. It also means making sure you understand—with absolute clarity—what others expect from you, even if they're not forthcoming with the information.

Failing to understand a client's expectations isn't an excuse for failing to meet those expectations. Failing to give your customers what they expect will cost you money, whether you know what they want or not. Isn't it better to know?

The best way to know is to ask, and then press for the answers.

That what Chelsea does. She likes to check in with her colleagues every now and then to ask if she is meeting their expectations. She created an easy-to-navigate online survey and sent it to seventy people who have used the support services her department offers. She invited them to fill it out anonymously so she would know what they liked, what they wanted but were not getting, and what she should stop.

She got only eight responses. That revealed that some of her colleagues might not be as accountable when it comes to clarity as Chelsea would like. But it doesn't mean she can't get clear about their expectations. So she pressed on.

Whenever she meets in-house "clients" one-on-one, she asks them those same survey questions. "It's a good conversation starter," she says. And it's way for Chelsea to be 100 percent accountable for meeting their expectations.

CLEAR AGREEMENT FORM

What is the **TASK?** What is the task or project I am taking ownership of?	
What is the **OUTCOME/ DELIVERABLE?** Consider • Level of detail? • Format? • Measures or standards? • Customer/end user of information, product, or service?	
What **ACTIONS** will I take to complete the task, project, outcome, or deliverable? Consider • Others involved? • Authority needed? • Assistance needed? • Resources needed?	
What are the **BY WHENs?** • What are the deadlines for this task, project, or deliverable? • How do we agree to renegotiate deadlines if needed?	
What are the **STAKES** associated with this task, project, or deliverable? • Benefits of completing? • Consequences of not completing? • Who will be affected?	

From *The Accountability Experience Participant Workbook*, by Linda Galindo (Pfeiffer, 2010)

CHAPTER

DAVE'S STORY

"Making a promise means keeping it, and that
includes a promise to yourself."

—*Dave Porter, CEO*

Dave recalls that he was a "knucklehead college kid" the
morning he borrowed a friend's suit and tie, rode the train
from Philadelphia to Washington, D.C., camped out at the
McPherson Square subway station, and waited for the White
House intern coordinator to emerge from the top of the cavern-
ous escalator on her way to work.

For weeks, Dave had left phone messages for the high-
ranking White House aide, but she never called him back.
So he set out to ask her in person to hire him to work in the
Ronald Reagan White House.

It took her less than a minute to say no. Dave understood
the woman's reluctance to offer a spot in the prestigious internship program to a West Chester University sophomore with
average grades, when plenty of top-rated Ivy League seniors
were begging her for the same job. So a couple of weeks later, he
boarded the train at dawn for his second unannounced trip to
the capital city.

This time, he talked faster. He said he would be the first
intern to arrive every morning and the last to leave at night. He

handed her his resume. He told her just how badly he wanted the job. She invited him to walk with her. A few weeks later, she hired him.

That wasn't the first time he took extraordinary measures to get what he wanted. Two years earlier, West Chester University also had rejected Dave when he applied for admission. He didn't tell his parents. Instead, he hopped into his beat-up old Gremlin and drove 147 miles from his parents' New Jersey home to West Chester, Pennsylvania, rejection letter in hand.

"I think you made a mistake," Dave told the admissions officer, who listened while Dave outlined the contributions he could make to the college. When he left for home twenty minutes later, he was an incoming freshman.

Dave takes the risks he needs to take to get the outcome he wants. He is accountable for his successes, and he does whatever it takes to accomplish his goals. He successfully won a spot in the freshman class and the coveted White House internship because he is accountable for fulfilling his ambition for success.

Indeed, every person has the ability to win what they want the same way Dave did—through personal accountability.

"If you say, 'This is what I want to do,' and you don't get there, ask yourself this question: 'Have I done every single thing in my power to get that opportunity?'" Dave advises.

By the time Dave turned thirty-five, he was president and CEO of Baystate Financial Services, one of New England's oldest and largest privately owned financial services firms. Under his watch, the Boston-based company has grown to a $100 million-a-year firm with 500-plus associates, including 275 financial advisors.

He attributes much of his success to his mindset of total accountability. He believes that making a promise means keeping it, and that includes a promise to himself. He lives a life of accountability for his promises, his decisions, his behavior, and his outcomes—good or bad.

That's Where Winners Live.

CHAPTER

TAKING 9 ACTION

> "Personal accountability is getting stuff done based
> on *me*. I am responsible for my performance and
> getting things done without looking or leaning or
> depending on other people. So if something goes
> wrong or right, it's all mine."
>
> —*Abigail Lechthaler, financial advisor*

Not everybody is as fearless as Dave, who begged a White House bigwig for an internship, but highly accountable people routinely take the risks and the actions they believe are necessary to earn their own happy endings.

For one person, that might mean adding an extra hour to her work day so she can take every other Friday off. For another, it might mean making cold calls—even though he'd rather have a root canal than contact strangers—so he can take his family to Hawaii by winning a quarterly sales contest.

For Brennan, it meant backing away from his less-ambitious friends. Brennan's idea of a good time is racing to the office in the morning to see if he can beat everybody else in.

"It's a healthy competition," says the twenty-six-year-old manager of the small group of early birds who typically arrive by 7 A.M., even if the day isn't shaping up to be busy. Meanwhile, most of Brennan's closest friends are sleeping off the party from the night before—youthful behavior from which he has distanced himself. "I think, 'Is your outside life getting in the way of being successful in your job?'" he says. "Mine isn't."

So those friends aren't so close any more. Neither are the guys who used to be his colleagues but now report to him. "I had to distance myself from these people on my team," says the young manager. "I don't want them to come back into the office the next day and say, 'Brennan was the life of the party last night.' Sure, I'll go out with them and have a couple of beers, but if I see things are going to get crazy, I bow out and say I have something else I need to do."

That's not easy. Brennan likes to party as much as his friends do. What he likes better, though, is his professional status, his paycheck, and his new reputation as a go-getter on his way to the top. So he is accountable for being at work early in the morning, keeping a clear head, making good decisions, and setting an example for his staff—which includes a few older people with more experience in sales.

He has empowered himself to back away from his fraternity-house social behavior in exchange for success. He is accountable for his success.

Some of his friends have made a different choice. They still drag themselves to their desks after too little sleep and too much alcohol the night before. Most of them earn less money and are not managers.

Who's to say the two opposing choices aren't equally accountable?

Maybe you figure you'll have plenty of time to run the rat race later in your career, so you might as well make after-work fun a priority while you can. Or you're a night owl and just don't want to wake up early. Or you'd rather be buddies with the guys at work than manage them and risk your friendships.

Maybe you don't want the life that Brennan has chosen. If that's your choice, there's nothing wrong with it. It's an accountable choice. Saying "no" to a promotion or early success is just as empowering as saying "yes." There's no shame in admitting that "early to bed, early to rise" doesn't make you happy—as long as you own your choices. Nobody is forcing you to forego the big salary and extra responsibility that Brennan has taken on, just as nobody forced him to take that on.

Brennan is accountable for his choice to back away from his friends. Likewise, you are accountable for your choice to work in a mediocre job.

And just as Brennan doesn't blame his job or his bosses for his choice to forfeit the "roaring" part of his twenties, someone who decides to embrace a more casual lifestyle at the expense of professional advancement has nobody but himself to point the finger at for a career that's not taking off.

Accepting the consequences of your choices—especially when others don't approve of them—can be difficult. But owning every decision—whether it's to focus on fun or to climb the corporate ladder—will, in the long run, help you feel good about your choices. The bonus: It will show others that you're making a conscious choice that's right for you. That will help the people around you respect those choices.

Those choices are empowering. In fact, "self-empowerment" is a critical step toward 100 percent personal accountability. Highly accountable people empower themselves to do what they have to do to get what they want. They don't wait for others to empower them; they know that's not how it works. They don't ask permission to reach for the stars or to sleep until noon if that's what makes them successful.

Highly accountable people empower themselves to find solutions to their own problems, to get the results they strive for, to step outside of their comfort zones and try new ideas or change their habits—all in their quest for success. They don't wait for success to happen; they make it happen by taking the risks and actions they believe will grease the wheels of their progress.

When they achieve what they want, they can take pride in knowing they empowered themselves to go and get it. When they fall flat, they are equally aware that they did it on their own, that their choices led them to an unwelcome result. Then they acknowledge it, figure out what went wrong, and empower themselves to try something else.

That's not what Cindy did when she accepted a sales position at a prestigious financial services firm, however. Cindy is resourceful and likes to figure stuff out on her own. In her eight years as the head of a small financial planning practice, that skill has paid off. She earned enough in commissions every year to qualify to attend most of her parent company's sales conferences. She can afford to live in a spacious, downtown loft; she takes cruises and European vacations; and she spends most winter weekends attached to her downhill skis.

To her, success means more than banking a big commission check every quarter. It means working as an entrepreneur, setting her own hours, working with and selling exclusively to doctors and other healthcare providers, and cultivating prospects through a network of acquaintances she has built up over the years.

The executives at her new company lavished her with praise and even expressed a hint of envy when they discussed her ability to identify and convert so many prospects in her chosen specialty. They sealed the deal with a $100,000 signing bonus, which will just about pay off the balance of the mortgage on her Vermont ski chalet. She happily accepted.

Three months later, she's not so happy. What happened? She doesn't fit into the culture at the new company, whose execs insist on reviewing call sheets every week to make sure everyone is contacting enough prospects. They like the sales staff to be in the office by 8 A.M. every day, and Cindy rarely makes that because she finds doctors are more available to meet for early morning coffee than for lunch. They recruited her for her stellar results, but now they're tampering with the process she follows to achieve those results. They're trying to squeeze her into a mold that's way too small for her.

For the first time in eight years, she hates her job. But if she leaves before she puts in a full year there, she will forfeit her signing bonus. So she talks her way out of the weekly checklist and does her best to keep her practice intact so she can run away from this company as soon as she can without returning her bonus. She is unhappy, stressed, and less productive in the meantime. She complains about her job and blames the executives who hired her for trying to undo her eight years of hard work.

That's often the reaction of someone who doesn't recognize that she alone is accountable for her status. She is accountable for her choice to keep the signing bonus and keep the job, even though she hates the latter. She could empower herself to return the money and find a more suitable practice. Yet she chooses to stay.

Like too many job candidates, Cindy did not empower herself to get clear about the culture of the new company or about the expectations of her new bosses. Recruiters are looking for successful people to add to their staffs. They're considering whether each candidate will fit in with the corporate culture. On the other hand, they typically don't consider whether the culture is a comfortable fit for the candidate.

When you apply for a job, you alone are accountable for deciding whether you can live in an inflexible culture of checks and balances or in one that's so unstructured you'll never be clear about the expectations. You are accountable for defining what success means to you and for deciding whether you can achieve it in the company's culture. And you are accountable for finding out if any of your new boss's "non-negotiables" are going to be a problem for you.

If you decide to accept a job that you wind up hating, or if you decide to keep a job that makes you unhappy, you are accountable. You can either empower yourself to adapt to the expectations and culture of the new place and make yourself happy there, or you can suffer silently and blame the recruiters for the bait they offered you—and the switch they made once you took it. Or you can empower yourself to quit.

Whatever you choose, be accountable for your decision. Be accountable for where you choose to work. Be accountable for the compromises you make.

Cindy once lived Where Winners Live. Not anymore. She has chosen to be a victim of her not-so-forthcoming new employers. She has the power to change it. Self-empowerment is available to her. It's her choice.

CHAPTER

DEFINING 10 SUCCESS

"I'm driven by success, not money. Success means
to me that I'm able to provide for my family in a
certain way. I want my children in the best schools.
It takes money to pay for that, but I'm not driven
by the money first."

—*Kareen Blake, financial advisor*

It has always been a priority for Cindy to exercise her independent, entrepreneurial spirit. It's part of her definition of success. Yet she abandoned that for a big signing bonus. That didn't work out so well for her.

Defining what success means to you—and keeping that definition at the top of your checklist when you make any important personal or career decision—will make you more successful. It also will make you happier.

Why accept a job that stifles your inner entrepreneur when you have defined "being an entrepreneur" as critical to your success? Why make a big signing bonus more important than working independently, when "signing bonus" isn't even a part of what you consider a key to your success?

It's unlikely that any two people define success in the same way. For some, success has a dollar figure: I will be successful if I earn $250,000 a year. Others define success as a lifestyle that the money can buy: Once I have a big house, a lakefront vacation home in Maine, and season tickets on the 50-yard line at Gillette Stadium, I'll know I'm successful.

Plenty of people aim higher: Success to me is owning a profitable company and running it my way. I am my own boss and employ a sales force of hundreds.

Kareen's definition of success isn't just about her career. It's as much about her personal life as it is about earning a comfortable living in sales. Kareen is a wife, mother, and business owner, but she doesn't think of herself as any one of those.

"All of those things are a part of me," says the forty-year-old financial advisor, who has worked in her field for thirteen years. "I don't define myself as just one or the other."

So before her two small children wake up every morning, she stares at herself in the mirror and repeats a definition of success that ties those roles together:

> "I am a spiritual person. God is an important part of my life and my family's life."
>
> "I am a committed wife in good times and bad."
>
> "I love my children unconditionally, even when times get tough."
>
> "I am a master producer and I will hit my income goal this year."

Kareen knows what she wants, so she is more likely to achieve it than someone who hasn't figured that out yet.

People who are stuck in dead-end jobs, careers that aren't suited for them, cities they don't care for, and marriages they know won't last often stay put, even though they are unhappy, because they don't know what else they want to do. If they devoted some time to examining their lives and looking to the future, they could set personal goals. They could define what success means to them. Then they would have something tangible to strive for.

If you want to succeed but you don't know what success is, you won't achieve it. Or you won't know it if you do achieve it. If you want to be successful, you need to know what "success" means to you. It's different for every person.

Spend some time pondering the meaning of success—in both your personal life and professional life. Sync the two definitions, and your quest for success will be more deliberate, organized, and achievable.

Your unique definition of success will reveal what is most important to you. To that end, you need to be completely honest with yourself about your intentions.

Is it more important to you to work for an organization that allows you to operate independently and feed your entrepreneurial spirit, or would you rather pocket a huge signing bonus, even if it means compromising your work style? Is it more important to make $250,000 a year, even if it means you have to work every Saturday, or would you prefer to live more modestly so you can spend weekends with your children while they're young?

It might be difficult to admit your choices. Maybe the money *is* more important to you than having freedom and flexibility in your job or spending weekends with your kids. Maybe you would do anything to achieve success as you define it, including lying, cheating, stealing, and exploiting others. Know that about yourself. Admit it, at least to yourself. It's yours.

Whatever makes you successful and fulfilled, be accountable for it. If you know what you want, you can go for it.

Defining success is most useful when you write it down, update it regularly as your circumstances and preferences change, and look at it every day. Give your definition of success a majority vote whenever you face a major decision.

If your definition of success includes spending Saturdays with your family, for example, assign that a hefty weight as you decide whether to go after a client who can meet only on Saturdays. If your success depends on a specific, steady income, let that guide your decision about whether to accept a job that pays commission only.

Your definition of success isn't a limitation. It's an honest statement of what you really want for yourself. That kind of statement can serve as an important reminder of what you value when your head gets turned by a temporary windfall that would require you to compromise your own success, as you define it.

Your unique definition of success is a springboard for you to answer this question: What is the gap between today and the day you are a success? If you define success as living in a 3,400-square-foot house and belonging to the country club, for example, ask and answer this question: What am I going to do to close that gap?

The sooner you define success, the sooner you will be successful. A guideline: Write a definition of success for each part of your life: professional, financial, health, home life, and community. Don't let anyone else influence you as you define it. Don't give away your power to decide exactly what success is for you.

WHAT IS YOUR PERSONAL DEFINITION OF SUCCESS?

1. What about your current job provides the most satisfaction?
2. What about your current job makes you feel professionally successful?
3. What kind of work atmosphere lets you thrive?
4. What kind of support—and from whom—would you need to be successful?

Based on your answers, write your professional definition of success. Write no more than four succinct sentences, and use the present tense. Example: *I am* a vice president, not *I will become* a vice president.

1. _____

   _____

2. _____

   _____

3. _____

   _____

4. _____

   _____

CHAPTER

11

ACCOUNTABLE FOR, ACCOUNTABLE TO

"At the end of the day, to be successful in this
business, you need—in the morning—to say, 'What
will I do today?' and at night to say, 'What didn't I
do?' Be honest with yourself."

—*Ann Swartz, chief operating officer*

Once you define success, you alone are accountable for achieving it or for choosing not to achieve it. You decide how, when, and if you bring that definition to fruition. That sharp focus can be what drives you toward a mindset of 100 percent accountability.

Highly accountable people clearly understand that they are accountable for their choices, whether the outcomes are good or bad. They also know precisely what they are accountable for and to whom they are accountable. That's part of their mindset.

Highly accountable people have a deep understanding of the consequences of their choices. Their mindset of 100 percent accountability comes, in part, from understanding the benefits of making accountable choices and the consequences of dropping the ball. Most often, those benefits and consequences are extremely personal. Your choices will inevitably affect what you cherish the most: your family, your reputation, your lifestyle, and even your health.

So as you craft your definition of success, keep in mind how the choices you make to achieve it—or not achieve it— will affect the people and things you hold dear. What are you accountable for other than achieving success as you define it? To whom are you accountable? Consider the following.

Your reputation. It took just four words from Bernadette, an experienced insurance agent, to destroy a four-year relationship with a client who had six policies worth $1 million-plus: "It's not my fault." In fact, Bernadette had accidentally checked the wrong box on an application for life insurance for a man who died two months later, and his death benefit was in question. His wife, who had expected to collect twice as much as she did, called Bernadette to find out why.

Instead of expressing her sympathy to the woman or offering to investigate the mix-up, she told the woman, who was emotional and angry when she called, "You can't blame me for this." The woman, who had hoped Bernadette would correct her mistake or at least look into what happened, canceled all of her policies and took her accusations to the state's insurance commission for investigation.

Better words for a woman who has just lost her husband and then learned he had inadequate insurance? "I'm so sorry for your loss. I'll try to help you."

To that client, and to anyone the client told about the incident, Bernadette is not a successful insurance agent with a thriving practice and good results. She is a woman with no compassion who denies she is accountable for her own mistakes.

But Bernadette is accountable for her reputation. She is accountable for overreacting and for saying the worst possible thing to her client.

Your word. If you don't do what you say you will do, your clients will not trust you. Even the smallest breach of an agreement can cancel a sale and turn away a client—even a long-time, loyal one.

Ed's definition of success is all about how much money he makes, so he is driven to sell as much as he can as fast as he can. Sometimes, his calendar is so jam-packed that he can't finish what he started in the time he allotted for it.

That's what happened when Shari met with him to go over her retirement portfolio. She wanted to drop any investments she had made in companies that use animals for product testing. Her commitment was genuine, even if her request wasn't urgent. Ed said he would research the companies in her portfolio and get back to her within a week.

Two weeks later, Shari called to ask for a progress report, and it took Ed, who intended to follow up with her but knew it wasn't urgent, three more days to return her call. By then, she had already approached another financial planner, who, eager for her business, had produced the research and won her as a client.

Shari's request wasn't a priority for Ed, because he knew it wasn't urgent. But it was important to Shari, who expected Ed to make good on his promise to do the research and call her back when he said he would. Ed is accountable for keeping his word. He is accountable for not keeping it, too.

Your public "face." When you walk into CEO Dave's office, you won't see a "Wall of Fame" covered with diplomas and trophies and certificates. Instead, you'll see photos of his five children and lots of golf memorabilia. If you sit down to talk with him, he's as likely to engage you in a conversation about skiing as he is to discuss your need for financial planning.

Dave wants people to know him as a family man, an avid golfer, and a man who enjoys hitting the slopes as much as he wants them to acknowledge his professional achievements. He wants the 500-plus people who work at his company to find him approachable, friendly, and interested. So he is accountable for nurturing that perception.

"Unless you are accountable to what that public perception is going to be, people aren't going to think that of you," he says.

If you're the fastest runner or the best basketball player, for example, people are going to think of you in that way. If that's what you want, then you are accountable for maintaining that reputation—by continuing to do whatever it takes to be the best.

Dave wants the public to think of his company as a growth organization. So he acts on that. He is accountable for growing the company and maintaining the public perception he wants.

Like many business professionals, Dave has embraced the Johari Window technique, which was created by Joseph Luft and Harry Ingham in 1955 to help people understand themselves and the way others perceive them. The Johari Window shows four "panes," or boxes. The top-left pane represents your public side. In a Johari Window exercise, you would fill that box with adjectives that describe yourself as you would like others to know you. You would include personal traits that you want others to see in you, so you make them public. The pane under that represents your private side, which you would fill with personal information that you know about yourself but withhold from most others. You would not want that information to become part of your public persona.

At the top-right corner of the box is your blind spot. Here, others would choose adjectives that describe how they perceive you. Often, you might not know this is what your colleagues, friends, or the public believe about you. Often, you would prefer that they stick to the public persona you created rather than filling in the blanks for themselves. The last pane, on the bottom right, is for the unknown or subconscious.

Jonathan, for example, has a big blind spot. He likes to be "the man" in the office. For years, he was a Top 25 financial advisor at his company, and his peers looked up to him as a role model. Young sales professionals sought his advice. Seasoned colleagues wanted him on their teams.

He worked hard and played hard. He earned an enviable income and made friends with everyone.

At some point, Jonathan decided his public reputation was so good that he no longer needed to work so hard. As his numbers slipped, his colleagues' opinions of him slowly started to slip as well. He had no idea. Once "the man," always "the man," he thought.

His CEO asked him, "Do you like being 'the man?'"

"I do. That's how people think of me," Jonathan replied.

"Since your production has slipped, people aren't thinking that way about you anymore," the boss said.

"Is that right? I didn't know."

In fact, Jonathan's production had become so mediocre that his colleagues no longer placed him on the pedestal where he enjoyed living so much. Jonathan had stopped nurturing his public persona. His perception was, "I'm the man." But he had a blind spot: To everyone else, he *used to* be "the man."

You are accountable for your public persona. And that means knowing your blind spot. To know your blind spot, you have to ask others what it is. And you might not like the answers.

For example, if your public persona is that you have an open-door policy and are willing to talk to anyone, but you don't look up from your iPhone when somebody walks into your office, your blind spot might be that people think your policy is insincere or that you don't have time for them.

The ultimate goal: to reduce that blind spot. Be accountable for knowing what your blind spot is. Then, if you become aware of your blind spot and you choose to ignore it, it becomes part of your public persona.

You choose how others perceive you. You are accountable for how others perceive you.

Your quotas. Sales is a numbers game, and sales professionals are accountable for hitting those numbers.

If your commissions already outpace your boss's expectations, you might get to define your own financial goals, and you are accountable for earning the income you want and the sales trips you covet. Maybe you want to work your way to a private office or you want to take your spouse on the Caribbean cruise that your company is dangling as the prize for next quarter's top seller. You are accountable for your success in reaching those goals.

More likely, you're accountable for selling enough to meet your company's expectation for someone in your position.

Blaming other people or circumstances beyond your control for falling short of your numbers won't help you meet those goals, whether they're self-selected or required as a condition of your employment. Empowering yourself to take the actions necessary to achieve those goals is the way to get it done.

Your company. Whether you own a business or work for someone else, you are accountable to your company and accountable for maintaining its reputation.

Jackie swore like a sailor, got into a lot of shouting matches, and had a hard time holding down a job. Still, she was able to impress a recruiter with her determination to change her life for the better and with her ambition to work in the legal field.

That was ten years ago. Today she works as a compliance officer in the highly regulated financial services field, and she has a mindset of 100 percent accountability for upholding her firm's good reputation.

"Maintaining relationships and presenting yourself to the public in a positive manner are all part of being personally accountable for your actions," says the thirty-year-old. "You have to understand that the decisions you're making determine how people will perceive both you and the firm you work for."

Your colleagues. The top-producing financial advisor at the firm where Charlotte works meets with clients whenever and wherever they want. And that means he calls Charlotte, the company's financial planning director, at all hours.

Charlotte works a daytime schedule, Monday through Friday. But when the top advisor calls her on Sunday afternoon with a request to help him prepare for a meeting he's having in five minutes, she takes the call.

"Whether I answer that question or not, I still get paid my salary," says Charlotte, who admits she has taken calls from frantic advisors as late as 2 A.M., as long as she believes they are not taking undue advantage or being disrespectful. "But it might make a difference to him in making a sale or not."

Once the advisor calls her for help, she says, she is as accountable for that sale as he is.

Plus, she is accountable for her choice of careers. "The hours are the hours, and that's part of the ebb and flow of business," she says. "If you want to show up at 9 A.M., sit at your desk, and clock out at 5 P.M., then you're in the wrong business. It is what it is."

Your clients. When Kerry sells an insurance policy, she sees the future.

The mother of two young children, Kerry thinks about the children of her clients who buy life insurance policies because the kids are the ones who will need and use the money in case of a tragedy. When someone asks about long-term care, she knows the policy will help keep her client's assets intact so his survivors—and not a nursing home—will benefit from them.

"I'm advocating for the children," she says.

Her philosophy: "Money is just a tool we use to do the things we want to do. So if my client can accumulate a lot of money, he can use that money as a tool . . . to give to charity or to give to his grandchildren, and to create a lifelong legacy."

To that end, Kerry always asks her clients a simple question: "What does money mean to you?" That, she says, is what drives every sale.

And if her philosophy means she has to see seventy clients instead of ten to produce the same amount of revenue for her company, she will. "I'm not going to drive the sale based on how much money I'm going to make," she says. "It's about how I treat that client. I want to make sure I'm doing a good job."

Plus, she knows if she does a good job, that client will personally recommend her to many others.

Your lifestyle. Janet's ideal workweek has just four days. So she draws a big red X over every Friday on her calendar to remind herself when her three-day weekend starts. Nevertheless, the investment advisor has worked every Friday for the past eighteen months, ever since she opened a second office.

It wasn't always that way, however. Janet's work ethic tells her that she doesn't have to work more hours to make more money if she uses her time efficiently. For years, she worked from 9 A.M. to 4 P.M., four days a week with great success. "The more effectively you work, the more successful you will be," she notes. "Anyone who tells you otherwise isn't doing it right."

Yet she's been "off" for going on two years. "I felt I needed Fridays to get caught up, but I really don't," she notes. So four months ago, she made a four-day week her top priority. And four months ago, she joined a "study group" of colleagues, all around her age and with similar levels of success at work, to hold her feet to the fire. She joined because the group's aim is to keep its members accountable. And this group is determined to keep Janet accountable to her resolve to live a balanced life by working only four days a week.

Janet is still working Fridays. But at least she's working toward a solution. "I don't want to report for the fourth month in a row that I failed myself," she says.

Your family. Perhaps the sharpest double-edged sword for the highly accountable sales professional is commitment to family.

Henry says he is accountable to his family. His second wife, who is fifteen years his junior, holds him accountable for earning enough money to maintain the comfortable lifestyle they have lived since she married him twelve years ago. A passionate salesman and a top seller at his firm, Henry has never had trouble earning hefty commissions to spend on a nice home, expensive vacations, private schools for the couple's children, and generous gifts.

After thirty years in the business, though, a middle-aged Henry has concluded that being accountable to his family means more than providing the things money can buy, especially now that he has a second chance to raise children.

"I work all hours, and I love to work. But I don't have as much time as I'd like to spend with my wife or kids, and I love them, too."

Henry had always measured his accountability to his wife and children in dollars and cents. So had his wife. Yet now that he is re-evaluating the "family" piece of his definition of success, time and experiences with his children while they are young are weighing more heavily. At least they are to him, and that is creating a problem in his marriage, because he wants to cut his work hours by 20 percent, which could pare his paycheck proportionately. His wife is not in favor of the change.

Henry has always been successful because he has had a clear definition of what success means to him and has had the mind-set of 100 percent accountability to that definition. So what happens when his definition changes?

Henry's choice: He continued to forfeit time with family in favor of the big paycheck. He decided his promise to provide a lavish lifestyle for his wife was a commitment he must keep, and that he could not do that if he scaled back at work.

Karen faced a similar decision a few years ago. The unmarried sales professional had everything: money, a spacious home, memberships in prestigious social clubs, friends all over the world. Her days and evenings were filled with meetings, lunches, golf games with clients, and opportunities for more success. Yet she was lonely, and at age forty-five, she adopted a toddler.

In a moment, her life changed. She was accountable to a child for the first time, and, like Henry, her definition of success needed revising. Karen decided to move to a less-pricey neighborhood so she could scale back her work hours, even though it meant she would forfeit commissions, trips, and rewards at work. Now the mother of a twelve-year-old, Karen notes: "Money never made me as happy as my little girl does."

Henry and Karen are equally accountable for their choices. In fact, how to balance work and family often is a family decision.

For those who work in sales, the job is a way of life. A spouse who doesn't buy into that concept is not going to support the sales professional's decision to work long hours and to be available to clients after hours and on weekends. Likewise, a spouse who counts on a partner's high income might not support his or her decision to take even a temporary punch in the paycheck to feed a non-work passion, such as volunteering for a charity, playing for a softball team, or caring for a sick parent.

In other words, your view of a balanced life might not jibe with your spouse's view.

For those who do not have families that depend on them, the balancing act is just as important. When you constantly put off friends, hobbies, personal goals, vacations, and downtime because you're working all the time, you will lose friends and these pleasurable activities.

Your definition of success will change as your life does: when you marry, have children, divorce, grow older, become a grandparent, or take an interest in something new. Incorporating those changes into your life as a sales professional—instead of pushing them aside because they are not work-related—will give you a better chance for success and could keep you from becoming bitter, resentful, or regretful later. Your definition of success could also stop you from rationalizing poor behavior or taking unethical shortcuts.

The fact is, you'll have nobody to resent but yourself. You are accountable for your choice to balance your work and life—or not.

Your conscience. Harvey attends a lot of funerals. Because he sells insurance, he's one of the first people a grieving client calls after a death or another tragedy. But he does more than file their claims. He holds their hands in the middle of the night while they wait for loved ones to arrive. He offers them advice about how to move forward. He even helps fill out insurance forms for acquaintances who are not his clients.

"I have an attitude that if you just do what you know is the right thing to do, the commissions and the fees all take care of themselves," he says.

And they have. Harvey has received calls from friends and relatives of bereaved clients who were impressed with his compassion during a crisis and want to do business with him because of it. He has volunteered for charities whose members later bought large amounts of insurance from him.

"You have to do things from your heart because you want to help, not because you expect to get business from it," he advises. "That will backfire."

WHAT IS YOUR BLIND SPOT?

Fill in three of the four panes of the Johari Window.

PANE 1. Your public persona. Choose five adjectives that you *would like* others to use when they think or talk about you.

1. _____

2. _____

3. _____

4. _____

5. _____

PANE 2. Your blind spot. Ask two trusted colleagues to write five adjectives each that reveal *how others* describe you. You might be surprised to learn that these adjectives are different from the ones you chose in Pane 1.

Colleague 1

1. _____

2. _____

3. _____

4. _____

5. _____

Colleague 2

1. _____

2. _____

3. _____

4. _____

5. _____

PANE 3. Write five adjectives or details about yourself that only your most trusted confidantes know and that *you would not want* to be part of your public persona. You might find that some of them showed up in Pane 2—even though you thought they were private.

1. _____

2. _____

3. _____

4. _____

5. _____

(Continued)

YOUR CHALLENGE: Sync Panes 1 and 2 so they are the same. Be accountable for your public persona by learning your blind spots and altering your behavior so you *are* the person you want others to think you are. Describe five ways you will eliminate your blind spots.

1. _____

_____

2. _____

_____

3. _____

_____

4. _____

_____

5. _____

_____

CHAPTER

DO WHAT YOU NEED TO DO

> "Everybody has twenty-four hours a day. You can
> do with it what you like. So whether you choose to
> browse the Internet, or hang out at lunch and chill
> out, or work, ultimately the fruits of your efforts are
> shown in your business. I'm accountable to myself."
>
> —*Jerry Facey, financial advisor*

Once you adopt a mindset of 100 percent accountability, you define what success means to you, and you understand to whom and for what you are accountable, you will be in the best possible position to determine what you need to do to get everything you want from your career and from your life.

Next step: Adopt a mindset of self-empowerment.

Nobody can empower you to become successful. Nobody can empower you to embrace a mindset of personal accountability. Nobody can empower you to make your dreams come true— except for you.

A boss at work can give you authority, permission, or resources to take the actions you need to take to accomplish a goal or finish a task. But only you can empower yourself to use those tools and act.

A colleague can help you reach a personal benchmark by offering advice or pitching in to do the work that will ease your way to a promotion or a big sale. But only you can empower yourself to ask for or accept that help.

A teammate can deny you access to information, a work product, or another person from whom you need something before you can accomplish your goal. But only you can empower yourself not to let that stop you from meeting your deadlines or impressing your clients.

Once you know what you want—for your day, your year, or your life—you have to work for it. Don't wait for it. Work for it.

Figure out what you have to do to get what you want. What kind of behaviors will make you successful, as you define that? What actions will you need to take to accomplish your goals for today and for your career? What risks are involved as you move from desiring success to pursuing it to having it?

Change requires action. Action involves risk. Risk has consequences. Those consequences are yours and yours alone.

Are you up for that?

Do you want what you want badly enough to act on it and to take risks to get it? Will you accept the consequences of those actions and risks, whether they are good or bad?

You already have the power to get what you want. This is self-empowerment.

Most sales professionals define their career success in terms of production. The more you sell, the more money you earn. The more money you earn, the more the company profits from your efforts, and the more its executives value you. The more the company values you, the greater your chance of promotions, rewards, trips, and other perks. And the higher your status in the company, the more attractive you will be to competitors who might offer even greater perks, and to potential clients who want to buy from the best and will help you keep your status as a top salesperson.

Likewise, many sales professionals define their personal success in terms of lifestyle. They know that selling more means being able to afford nice homes, exotic vacations, the best schools for their children, and a comfortable retirement.

That kind of success requires action and risk.

Clark was up for it. Fresh out of business school, the twenty-four-year-old landed a position as an advisor with a top financial services firm and set his sights on a six-figure salary.

He invested in a couple of sharp business suits, rose before the sun every morning, worked a minimum of eight hours a day, talked friends and family into buying from his company, and cold-called or qualified prospects for at least four hours a day.

Then he closed his first sale. And his second, his third, and his twentieth. The commissions poured in, and this young go-getter was on his way.

But he didn't earn six figures. By the end of his first year, after dropping out of his Saturday-morning softball team so he could meet with clients, and after skipping his family's annual vacation so he could attend a sales training seminar, he pocketed $66,000 from a combination of his commissions and a small salary.

Disappointed that he missed his personal goal of $100,000 in his first year, Clark woke up before light, pulled on his suit, and drove to work with a new goal on the first day of his second year in the financial services business: $132,000—double his first year's take.

He had been warned: Inexperienced newcomers to this kind of selling can consider a first-year salary in the mid-$60,000 range a success. After a few years with the organization, he could earn more than $200,000 of field and commission revenue—and earn his company a profit of $80,000.

That is, if he were willing to make personal sacrifices such as giving up Saturday mornings to work and skipping fun in favor of professional development.

In fact, if he doesn't reach that revenue goal within a few years, he can expect to have a serious conversation with his manager about how well suited he is for a sales career. About 40 percent of financial advisors achieve that industry benchmark within the first few years. The remaining 60 percent either earn at a slower pace or figure out sales is not for them.

Clark had been advised by his company's top earners, who see success through a lens of dozens of years in the business: It can take a beginner forty cold calls, five days a week, into a promising market to get in front of good prospects ten to twelve times a week. If you schedule ten appointments, one to three of those potential clients will buy from you. As you get better in the business, that formula improves, sometimes so much that four out of every five people you talk to will become clients.

So Clark is willing to put in the time, make the personal sacrifices, glue his seat to his chair, contact and meet with as many prospects as he can, and ask for the sales. It's his commitment to his definition of success: to build a career that will pay him six figures a year. He has empowered himself to take the action (forty calls a day, ten meetings a week, asking for the sale), the sacrifices (working Saturday mornings, skipping vacations), and the risks (falling short of his short-term goals, earning commissions but no salary starting in Year Four) to be successful as he defines that.

He is empowering himself to do what he needs to do to get what he wants.

Eleven Pearls

Following are eleven pearls from financial services sales professionals who earn six figures a year—and from some who approach seven.

1. You will work your tail off during your first three years as a sales professional.

Just as Clark discovered, it takes more than forty hours a week to build a client list, get a feel for your own selling style, learn about your product, and figure out how to close a sale. It also takes dedication and personal sacrifices. And it probably won't make you rich—at least not for the first couple of years.

Keep your focus on your definition of success. With experience, the money will come. For the inexperienced, however, the first few years can be a struggle.

Here's a tip: Map out your ideal week. How many people will you see? How many phone calls will you make? How will you spend your time? High-level sales executives estimate that you'll need to devote 80 percent of your time during your first three years to "activity": contacting prospects, booking appointments, and meeting with potential clients. Without that constant activity, you're unlikely to hit your numbers.

So if you choose to work with doctors, for example, schedule ample time at the local hospital. If you want to sell to home builders, attend every meeting of the local home builders association.

How much time are you spending on the activities that will help you make your numbers and meet your goals? If you want to be a top salesperson and a high earner, it takes time and activity to reap the rewards.

Executives treat high producers differently. Nobody tells the sixty-year-old sales professional who earns $1 million a year how many people he needs to call each week or what time he has to get to work.

If Clark decided to rent a home on Cape Cod for six weeks this summer, he would probably lose his job, because there would be no way for him to meet his sales quotas while he was gone or to catch up on them when he got back.

But the golden salesperson who earns seven figures can do what he wants. His numbers so far exceed what's required that he can take a month and a half off without coming anywhere close to jeopardizing his standing.

He also easily qualifies for the company-sponsored trips to Disney World, Italy, and Australia.

Stay focused on activity that will produce results, and you'll be sitting on the plane next to Golden Boy during those trips.

Choose to slack off, complain, and blame circumstances beyond your control for your poor showing, and you'll be dropping your wealthy colleague off at the airport instead.

2. It takes action to make sales.

Don't wait for would-be clients to find you. Invest in prospecting lists. Make cold calls. Attend functions where you can meet the kind of people who will buy your products and services. Approach your personal contacts, such as friends, family, former classmates, and past colleagues. Join online social networks. Introduce yourself to strangers. Ask for meetings. Listen to every person you come into contact with—at work, at social functions, at the school bus stop where you wait with your children every morning—to hear if they might have a need you can fill.

3. Very few of those people will buy anything.

Here's a rule of thumb in the financial services industry: If you contact forty people every day, every week, you might make only one sale a week. So contact more than forty people. Be diligent about making new contacts, even as you work on closing multiple sales. Never stop contacting new prospects.

4. Cold-calling is effective.

Even many seasoned, successful sales professionals would rather suffer through a root canal than pick up the phone and call a stranger, but it's much quicker to get in touch with forty people via phone than to drive to each of their offices. Be patient and persistent. Industry research shows it takes an average of fourteen tries to make contact with a prospect, so if you give up after leaving only four or five voicemail or e-mail messages, you're cutting your would-be clients off too soon.

5. Before you talk to potential customers about a product, learn about their need for it and their experience with it.

Ask your prospects if they are satisfied with the person from whom they already buy the products or services that you represent. Someone who works as a financial planner, for example, would ask the following:

- Do you already have a financial advisor?
- How did you meet your advisor?

- What do you like or dislike about the advisor?
- Would you recommend this advisor to others?
- What products does the advisor recommend?
- Does the advisor charge a fee or earn a commission?

6. Your company has expectations for how much you sell. Know what they are.

An advisor at Baystate Financial Services, Clark is young, and his income goal, for now, is in the low six-figure range. But his company will expect him to earn more than that after a few years, because the more he earns, the more the company earns. So his managers will coach him, push him, and require him to reach beyond his original goal.

An average-earning financial planner with a few years of experience earns about $218,000 every year, and top advisors take home half a million dollars or more. An experienced Baystate planner who settles for a $100,000 paycheck is considered below average.

No matter what industry you sell in, you will be required to hit the company's numbers. Adjust your goals to match or exceed those of your employer.

7. Executive-level sales managers are willing to share the selling process that made them rich—because they believe it will make you rich, too. Run *with* it, not away from it.

In fact, managers often prescribe a process for you to follow on your way to hitting the company's numbers. It likely involves calling a certain number of people a day, meeting with a specific number of clients a week, and closing a defined number of sales every quarter. It almost certainly will require you to keep track of how many calls, meetings, and sales you have made, and to report that every week to your supervisor.

The process these selling superstars are so willing to share has already catapulted them into the money, and they will virtually guarantee you that it will work for you, too. Give it a try before you push it aside in favor of testing your own unique strategy. Once you have satisfied the higher-ups that you can hit your numbers every quarter, you will have more leeway to create your own process for continued success.

8. Consider focusing on a niche client base.

If you concentrate your efforts on working with doctors, lawyers, home builders, or teachers, for example, make yourself an expert on the particular insurance and investment needs— or whatever your specialty—of people in that profession. Visit them where they work; know their schedules and when it is convenient to meet.

Do a litmus test: Qualify fifty people in your specialty area and contact them to ask for appointments. This will help you gauge how well this market suits your personality, your selling style, your schedule, and your knowledge of the industry.

9. Ask for personal recommendations.

Nearly every client that financial advisor Harvey works with has come to him via a personal recommendation from another client.

The reason: He asks for them.

He tells his clients up front that they can buy their insurance from any of thousands of people in the business. He shows them that the difference between those people and him is the level of customer service he offers, including round-the-clock access and regular, personal visits.

He also asks them to introduce him to three of their friends, neighbors, family members, or colleagues. If he doesn't get the list, he calls to ask for it again. "I'm not bashful about asking for personal recommendations," he says.

10. Ask for the sale.

The most common reason a prospect who seems like a sure thing doesn't buy is because nobody asked him to buy. Don't wait for the customer to offer to buy. When the time is right, clearly and confidently ask for the sale.

11. Ask for help.

The three most-important words might be, "I love you." But the four most-important words are, "Can you help me?"

Dave didn't know anybody near him in the bleachers of the auditorium where he sat watching his preteen daughter graduate from the eighth grade. He struck up a conversation with the woman next to him and learned she was a toxicologist, new to town, and hadn't made many friends since the move. Her husband, she said, had a PhD in life sciences and worked for a pharmaceutical company.

"Can you help me?" Dave asked the woman.

"Sure," the toxicologist responded, clearly pleased to be able to help a potential new friend.

"What does life sciences have to do with pharmaceuticals? I don't know what your husband's job would be."

The woman explained, and then she asked Dave what type of work he did. He told her about his job as a financial planner and insurance salesman.

"Oh!" she replied. "Can you help *me*?"

She's been a client ever since.

If you and a friend are walking along a busy street on your way to a restaurant, and someone stops you to ask for help, agree to help. Emotional reciprocity goes a long way. When you understand what motivates people—how you can help people and how they can help you—you will better understand what drives them.

People like being asked for help. If the CEO asks a twenty-six-year-old, second-year employee to help him with something as trivial as carrying a heavy box, that young employee might enjoy the chance to talk one-on-one with the Big Cheese. If the CEO asks the young associate to introduce him to someone who lives in the associate's hometown, it could connect employee and boss in a significant way, especially if the introduction leads to a sale.

Asking for help is a way to help yourself. It can help you be 100 percent accountable. In fact, few highly accountable people stay at that level without a little help from their friends.

Surround yourself with people who are willing to help you on your journey to the place Where Winners Live. Surround yourself with people whom you are willing to help on the same journey.

If you're earning $200,000 today and want to make $300,000 next year, tell this to someone you trust. Ask that person to help you make a plan. Choose a person who is highly accountable and will hold you to his or her high standards.

Choose a mentor or a group for mutual support. Report your goals, your progress, and your missteps. Ask them to suggest ways you can improve and succeed.

Highly accountable people ask for help when they need it. As you follow these eleven pieces of advice, keep your mindset of 100 percent personal accountability.

- Don't make excuses for not calling forty people a day.
- Don't blame the client for a lost sale if you never got around to asking for it.
- Don't throw your hands up and say, "I can't do this." That is a choice to fail.
- Don't offer reasons why your success isn't happening. That is a choice for it not to happen.
- Don't leave your success up to chance. If you believe 50 percent of your chance for making a sale is up to you and 50 percent is up to circumstances beyond your control, that is a choice to fail.

For every young sales professional who is successful, there's another who can explain why she couldn't get the job done. The difference between them is mindset.

The only secret to success in the sales profession is personal accountability. What you do determines how much you sell.

Make calls—lots of them. Schedule appointments. Meet clients. Ask for the sale.

If you do these things, you will succeed.

It's like high-risk surgery. If your surgeon tells you to lose forty pounds so he can operate on you, and then you show up in the operating room heavier than ever, he can't guarantee that things will go well.

If you spend your working hours with a laser-sharp focus on the activity that is proven to reap sales, you will sell more, earn more, and achieve more.

You will live Where Winners Live.

13
FINE-PRINT ACCOUNTABILITY

> "Don't count on a lack of clarity to get a deal done.
> If you have any radar whatsoever that you're living
> on hope, you need to take action. Hope is not a
> plan."
>
> —Linda Galindo, *accountability thought leader,
> speaker, coach, consultant, author*

Jane lost the license she needs to sell securities and work as an investment advisor because she didn't know when it expired. The licensing agency didn't remind her to renew it. The securities broker whose products she sells didn't notify her of its expiration date. The compliance group at the financial services firm she's affiliated with didn't bring it to her attention.

"It makes my blood boil," says Jane. "The ball got dropped. I thought it was someone else's responsibility to track my licensing. Nobody will help me get it back."

Wait. There's more.

"I thought the license was good to go, even though I'd never done any continuing education credits."

Jane is prohibited from selling certain products in certain states without that license. To get a new one, she has to take a lengthy test. Tests make her anxious, and now she's losing sleep. In fact, she says, "I'm losing my mind over this."

So instead of taking the test, she's suffering a loss of business, income, and peace of mind.

She realizes that she needs to keep track of the expiration dates on all of her required licenses from now on, even though some of the companies she's affiliated with have said they will do it for her.

"That's what got me into trouble in the first place," she admits. "Somebody said, 'We'll keep track of this for you,' and I said, 'Hallelujah!' I can never trust that again."

This is a new mindset for Jane—from zero accountability to 100 percent accountability. Too bad it took losing her professional license, spending a lot of time and energy resolving the problem, and forfeiting who knows how many clients to get there.

But her experience is common. Think about how often you delegate your responsibility for something extremely important to someone you don't even know or to a faceless company whose policies you don't understand. Whether it is a credit card statement of conditions, terms, and policies, or the brochure that comes with a prescription notifying you of the medicine's potential side effects, the devil is in the fine print. We are surrounded by fine print, so much so that we rarely read all of it. Or any of it.

Instead, we blindly trust the company or the representative we're dealing with to make sure everything's in order. We sign our names under the line that says, "I accept the terms and conditions," even though we don't know what the terms and conditions are. However, that doesn't mean you are not accountable if something goes wrong.

If you get sick, for example, and your health insurance doesn't cover your illness, you are accountable for your lack of insurance, whether you understood the coverage or not. If an "early payment fee" shows up on your credit card statement and you didn't know about the penalty because you decided not to read the fine print, you are accountable. If your boss puts you on probation for ignoring company policies outlined in the associate handbook you never read, you are accountable.

It's not easy or pleasant to admit, after you learn of a negative consequence of your own negligence because you didn't read the fine print, that you are accountable. It seems unfair, and you might feel like a victim. And most of us can agree that we're all too busy to study all of the fine print that bombards us every day, and that we wouldn't understand most of it if we did bother to read it. Instead, we figure we will deal with it when the time comes—and, frankly, most of us believe the time will never come.

But it might. And when it does, you will be accountable for your choice to delegate responsibility to someone else for something that person really has no responsibility for.

There is a solution: Be proactively "fine-print accountable." Take back the power that comes with knowing what you are signing and choosing to agree to—or disagree with. And if you are the bearer of fine print—that is, if you are selling something that comes with conditions, terms, and exceptions that your buyers will not know about unless they read all of the fine print—be 100 percent responsible for making sure that customer reads and understands those terms and conditions. You'll save a lot of time and trouble later if you take that step up front.

Fine-print accountability involves three steps:

1. If you are signing or agreeing to something and don't have time to read the fine print—or you don't understand what it says—ask to speak to someone who can explain it to you. If you are selling something with lots of considerations included in the fine print, insist on reviewing these items with the customer, associate, or vendor before closing the sale.

2. Revisit the fine print occasionally. Terms and conditions change over time. Banks, insurance companies, and credit card companies routinely send out disclaimers, changes to privacy policies, and notices of fee increases via mail or e-mail, and you're expected to know about them and take

action if you object. Yet they come in the form of brochures printed in such small type that you would need a magnifying glass to read it. Similarly, if you are a service provider and your product's or company's terms and conditions change, enlarge the font size, simplify the language, and send out the information in a more consumer-friendly format that encourages your valued customers to read it and helps them to understand it.

3. Whether you're a buyer or a seller, make a list of the fine-print details you need to keep on top of, and commit to spending a few hours once a quarter reviewing, updating, questioning, or acting on them.

Your accountability for what's included in the fine print doesn't depend on whether you read it or understood it. You are accountable. Period.

14

I'M SORRY, BUT . . .

"The number one way to be accountable: not
assuming you know everything. It's OK to make
mistakes. I didn't get to where I am today by doing
everything right."

—*Caitlin DeSoye, director of financial planning*

College interns who work at Baystate Financial Services are
required to submit to the CEO a weekly summary explaining
what they accomplished and what they learned. These summaries are due on Fridays by 5 P.M.

One Friday, the summer's most promising part-timer got so
busy with work that she didn't submit her summary on time. She
sent it early Monday morning with a note that said, "I'm sorry
this is late, but I was so busy I couldn't get it done on Friday."

"I'm sorry, but . . ."

How many times do you hear that in a day?

This intern is just beginning her career, and she's already
apologizing for her decision to miss a deadline. Not a great way
to start a career in sales.

And it *was* a decision. Why apologize for being busy? Why
apologize for your decision? Are you saying you made the wrong
decision? You're an adult. Don't apologize. You're conscious of
the decisions you make. The reality is that you knew what you

were doing. The intern could have decided to stop being busy for a few minutes on Friday and send in her report on time, but she decided not to do this. She didn't want to do it. Is she really sorry?

Apologizing to the boss doesn't get the report turned in on time. Apologizing to yourself doesn't get you to the gym in the morning.

Apologies are hollow. In most cases, you really don't need to bother apologizing.

Saying "I'm sorry, but . . ." seems to prove you are not sorry. "But" what?

"I'm sorry I said you were a jerk, but you were acting like a jerk."

So why are you saying you're sorry? You clearly meant it. You chose to say it.

"I'm sorry I had a bad year, numbers-wise, but I have a million excuses."

I'm sorry you had a bad year, too, and I can tell you why you did: You have a million excuses.

"I'm sorry I missed our appointment, but something came up."

Skip the "I'm sorry, but...." Get the report in on time next week. Have a better year. Don't miss any more appointments.

Be accountable.

Listen to people who refuse to own their actions:

I'm sorry we'll never be able to retire, honey, but it looks like our Social Security payments won't be enough to support us.

(This has nothing to do with the couple's decision to borrow against the equity in the house and to take lavish vacations instead of saving for the future, does it?)

I'm sorry I'm late for work every day, but I live so far away that I can't get to the city on time.

(Why don't you choose to live a little closer in or to wake up earlier in the morning?)

"I'm sorry" reveals more to people than your lack of account-ability. It diminishes your credibility and their perception of your worth.

So stop dancing the "I Ain't Good Enough Cha-Cha."

How often do you apologize every day?

- I'm sorry I couldn't make it to the meeting.
- I'm sorry I didn't complete the assignment.
- I'm sorry I didn't return your call.
- I'm sorry for being late from the break.
- I'm sorry I have to leave early.

Remove the "I'm sorry" from each of these apologies. Once you do, these statements have power they did not have before: the power of personal accountability that is essential to demon-strating that you are a competent professional.

- I didn't make it to the meeting.
- I didn't complete the assignment.
- I didn't return the call.
- I own my choices and my behaviors.

Apologies too often come across as self-deprecating behav-ior. If you're constantly sorry for your behavior, your comments, or your decisions, it sounds an awful lot like you think they—and you—are not good enough.

Get a grip! If you don't think you're good enough, who will? People typically won't think any more of you than you think of yourself.

With your self-deprecating negativity, you are demonstrating to others how they should treat you. How is that good for you?

Never, ever self-deprecate.

Too many of us are unaware of the damage that subtle put-downs can do—whether they're aimed at ourselves or at others.

Expressing your lack of confidence in yourself can bring swells of agreements and commitments—and sales—to a stop.

So why do we do it?

Your parents might have taught you not to boast or stand out from the crowd. Teachers and clergy might have convinced you that humility is a virtue. You've learned since a young age that if you work hard and behave, you'll reap rewards.

Or maybe you think that putting yourself down keeps you safe from criticism. You do it before someone else can.

If I'm not good enough and I make sure you know that, my poor performance is understandable. I might even get some compliments or sympathy out of it.

That's great, if that's what you're after.

But if what you want is respect, frequently saying, "I'm sorry" won't do the job.

- I'm sorry. I don't understand this.
- I'm sorry. I probably did this wrong.

How often do you begin a statement with, "I'm sorry?" Keep track. You might be shocked. You might not even realize that you say it so often.

Try this experiment for one week: Preface every suggestion, proposal, or opinion with a positive statement.

- This is a brilliant idea, and I can't wait to share it with you.
- This is so good, you're going to want to give me a raise for thinking of it.
- I am excited about providing this input.

You have a lot to offer. Why would you want to diminish your contribution or your influence in any way with excuses, habitual apologizing, or uncertainty? Display your self-confidence and self-worth by dropping any hint of self-deprecation. Speak your worth plainly and clearly.

Ridding your conversations of "I'm sorry" will give you more personal power. Removing "I'm sorry, but . . ." will demonstrate your personal accountability.

If you truly believe you have something to be sorry about, choose to change your habits so you don't.

Part II

ACCOUNTABILITY AND TEAMWORK

CHAPTER

OWN YOUR COMPROMISES

"Be true to yourself, and never compromise your
values or your ethics. And work smart. You're going
to work hard, but you have to work smart."
—Ann Swartz, *chief operating officer*

One of many upsides to being 100 percent accountable is that you will feel sorry or regretful far less often for the choices you make.

Highly accountable people make choices based on the outcomes that they desire. Good choices lead to good outcomes. Good choices rarely lead to regret. And on the off-chance that those choices wind up leading to poor outcomes, the accountable sales professional stands up and owns them anyway.

That's not always easy, especially for someone who makes choices based on what should be rather than on what is. That person is going to be sorry all the time.

Cecilia is sorry she ever relied on her team leader, Grant, for anything. She blames him for the poor performance evaluation she just got from the CEO. She was so livid with Grant and her CEO because of that evaluation that she marched straight over to the office of the human resources director to complain about it.

The CEO had berated her for continually missing deadlines. He told her she is accountable for her poor evaluation, even though it is Grant, who reports directly to the CEO, who doesn't get his part of the work finished on time, and that's what holds Cecilia up.

"My performance evaluation is affected by something I cannot control," Cecilia complained to HR Director. "My work product, including meeting my deadlines, depends on the work of someone who reports directly to the CEO, and that person never provides me with what I need on time. And that person is not held accountable.

"So why is the CEO saying I am totally accountable for getting a poor evaluation and for missing those deadlines?"

The question was loaded. So HR Director asked Cecilia, "Have you talked directly to the person who does not give you what you need?"

"Yes," Cecilia replied. "He basically told me, 'Tough. You are not the boss of me.'"

HR Director pressed on. "Have you gone to the CEO directly about this?"

"Oh, no," Cecilia admitted. "If I did that, there would be retribution."

Fair enough. HR Director's next question: "Is the CEO aware of this person's lack of performance and he seems to be allowing it?"

"Yes."

"How long has this been going on?

"Three years."

Cecilia wanted HR Director to step in, to convince the CEO to hold Grant accountable and to revise Cecilia's performance evaluation so it reflected that the problem is not her fault. But HR Director took a different viewpoint. Here's why: Working for a CEO who will not hold someone else accountable is a choice. The CEO is not going to change. The person who does not give Cecilia what she needs on time in order to do her work is not going to change.

Cecilia has chosen to work for an organization where it's not possible to get a stellar performance evaluation unless these people change. That is not going to happen. She predictably experiences conflict because she is held accountable for something she does not believe she is responsible for. And Cecilia has known that for three years.

It is unfortunate that the CEO didn't come right out and tell Cecilia, on the day she was hired, that her ability to do her work would depend on others who would not be held accountable, and that she would be unlikely to qualify for pay increases because the people on whom she must depend do not do their work. Too bad he didn't tell her she would be paid to do her best, to be frustrated, and then to continue to do her best despite her frustration.

But in three years' time, she finally has figured it out. Her reaction, "It's not my fault," isn't getting her work done. It's not reaping her any positive performance evaluations. And it's certainly not convincing anyone to give her a pay raise.

Living on Planet What Should Be isn't going to change Cecilia's situation.

"But we're supposed to be a team," Cecilia objected.

"Supposed to be?" HR Director asked.

"Well, Grant and I should be working together and he should take my deadline into consideration before he misses his."

"You're right. He should."

HR Director was happy enough to acknowledge that Cecilia was right: Things should be different. But being right doesn't change the situation. Full accountability for the situation, in fact, comes in this statement: "I have done what I can. I have talked to those I am willing to talk to. And I accept this role in exchange for pay."

HR Director's last piece of advice: Shift to full accountability for what you are choosing now. If that choice is to tolerate more of the same, if it's to stay here and work with these people, own your choice.

Cecilia, of course, didn't like what she was hearing: She is 100 percent accountable for her poor performance evaluation. She is accountable for her unwillingness to talk to the CEO to try to resolve her problem with Grant. She is accountable for staying in a job where things aren't as she believes they should be. She is accountable for tolerating these conditions in exchange for her paycheck.

Whether she is making the right decisions or the wrong ones doesn't have anything to do with the fact that she is accountable for them.

Remove the good, bad, right, and wrong. Remove what should be or shouldn't be. All that remains is clarity. Cecilia is totally, personally accountable, whether the results are good or bad.

What are you doing in exchange for money that's making you unhappy? Identify it and act on it. It's your choice.

CHAPTER

THE BOSS OF YOU
16

> "Accountability is not just a one-stop shop. If you're accountable and you're successful, it's a win-win for everybody. You do get all you want."
> —*Harvey Lazarus, financial representative*

Cecilia chose to keep her job at the company where the CEO refuses to hold his "favorites" accountable for their inefficiencies. And she has figured something out: If the CEO won't hold her team leader accountable, she and her teammates could choose to do it.

Her seven-year-old niece taught her that lesson. A few weeks after her unhappy meeting with HR Director, Cecilia took her three young nieces out to shop and run errands one afternoon, and she promised them that they would all have ice cream if everyone behaved. She explained what that meant: They were each accountable for making sure nobody ran off out of sight, that all of them behaved respectfully while they were in the stores, and that every member of their little group worked together to get the errands done. As a group, the family would be accountable for cooperating and finishing the chores. The reward for that result, she told the girls, was ice cream.

One of the children pushed back. "Hey, that's not fair," she objected. "I can't control Emily. If she runs off, why will I get punished with no ice cream?" The comment startled Cecilia with the realization that the objections of this seven-year-old were basically the same as those she voiced to HR Director.

With sudden clarity, Cecilia explained to her niece that every member of the four-person shopping team that day would be accountable not just for themselves, but for the whole group. They would get their errands done, she would be less stressed, and that would earn them all a treat.

"But you are the grown-up," her niece declared. "We can't control our little sister."

"Your sister is standing right here and can hear me just as clearly as you can," Cecilia retorted. Then she looked right at the youngest and asked, "Do you understand that we are all accountable to get along, stay together, and get our errands done, and then we will have ice cream?"

Without hesitation, the youngest looked at the complaining sister and said, "That means you are not the boss of me; we are all the boss of each other."

Cecilia thought about posting that at the top of the next "team" meeting agenda at work. She realized that the hallmark of a true team is that the group doesn't need a boss to handle tardiness, poor performers, or personality conflicts. Teams support a team leader (one of their choosing is best) and hold each other—and that leader—accountable as they focus on results.

A high-performing team has a goal, a clear definition of success, clear roles, and the trust to depend on each other to get the job done. Each team member values every other member's contribution. Each team member understands the consequences of not holding up his or her end.

When there's a breakdown—such as a team leader who doesn't meet the group's agreed-upon deadlines—the team handles it. There's no running to the CEO or HR director. Instead, the team joins to support the offending member with earnest offers of help and reminders of the consequences when one "cog in the wheel" falters—such as missed project deadlines and poor evaluations for those who depend on that colleague to satisfy their own obligations.

That is a high level of personal accountability—both individually and collectively. And that kind of high-performing team is rare. Create that kind of a team for your next project, and your work experience will be transformed.

That's not so easy, to be sure. Team members are often chosen for you, so you can't pick and choose. And it can be infuriating to be on a team of goofs you did not choose.

When Cecilia dropped off her nieces at home after their afternoon together, the youngest girl ran to her mother to announce, "Aunt Cecilia told us we were accountable, and no one was the boss of me, and we got ice cream!"

If you and your teammates didn't need anyone to be "the boss of you," what reward would you get? Success? Satisfaction? More freedom or authority? Less stress? Better performance evaluations?

Be the boss of your own success, even if you work for someone else.

CHAPTER 17
TRUE TEAMWORK

"When it comes to teamwork, I can admit that
I'm not great at it. When it comes to my business,
it's like my household. I don't want somebody else
folding my laundry. I know what I like and where it
goes."

—*Abigail Lechthaler, financial advisor*

A mega-financial services company recently announced to associates that, effective immediately, everyone would be part of a team. The reasoning, the execs explained, is that the team approach to selling insurance and financial planning services has become more profitable than the individual approach.

The company's high-level producers responded to the news uniformly: "No way."

Among them was Patrick, who earned in the neighborhood of $450,000 last year in commissions. "I'm a top earner *because* I work individually," Patrick objected. "*I* find my own prospects. *I* cultivate them into clients. *I* close the sales. And *I'm* not about to share my commissions with anyone."

The execs countered: In today's marketplace, we simply have too many products with too many ins and outs for any individual to keep up with it all. Consumers are more demanding and less willing to wait for a specific person to get an answer or make a decision. We as a company have to be able to offer ready answers, even when the lead salesperson is unavailable. Teamwork prevents bottlenecks. It retains customers. It allows us to serve the customers 24/7.

Patrick stood his ground. "I would rather work individually than on a team, and your new rules are going to send me and my $450,000 in commissions to your competitor, where I can sell in a way that is comfortable and profitable and has always worked for me."

His colleague, Debra, also objected but without making a sound. The $300,000-a-year advisor agreed to embrace the new mandate for teamwork, yet she doesn't intend to share the spoils of her success any more than Patrick does. So she does what she has always done: She finds prospects, nurtures them, closes sales, and collects her commissions. But now she feels free to lob the tedious and even some of the tough parts of her routine onto lower paid "teammates," while she continues to pocket the profits and sign up for the exotic trips available only to high earners.

If she's a member of a team, your mother is an astronaut.

In business, most people use the word "team" too loosely. The term requires clarification.

Does "team" mean one person does all of the selling and the other team members do whatever she says? Does it mean a manager sets goals and assigns specific, independent tasks to each person in his group? Or does it mean a leader compiles the team, explains the assignment, and leaves the teammates to work together to get it done?

"Team" means different things to different people. Sometimes, it means different things to the same person, depending on the task at hand. Define before you assign. Know what "team" means to you—and let each team member know it, too.

Confusion over what constitutes a team is rampant in all kinds of professions. Consider the surgeon who must rely on his team of anesthesiologists and nurses for a successful surgery, yet wants everyone to do exactly as he demands. Or a basketball superstar, who expects the other four players on the court to set the picks and toss him the ball so he can take all of the shots—and claim all of the glory—himself. Or consider the team of students that takes on a group project, yet only a couple of them—those to whom the A grade is most important—do almost all of the work because those who would be happy with a C are more than willing to let them.

Those aren't teams. They're groups of people tasked with the same assignment, but there's no teamwork involved, no collective effort, no joint ownership of the result. On a true team, each member is 100 percent accountable for the success of the group and for the outcome of its task. If you don't buy that, consider the "team" that's responsible for the fire insurance policy you bought on your home.

Suppose you initiated a call to an insurance representative you have never met, because you bought an investment property in a state where your regular agent isn't licensed. The two of you discuss your need to insure the condominium that you plan to rent out, and her staff and the company's underwriters get the policy in place. You arrange with your mortgage company to pay the premiums, and when you file a small claim after a faulty water heater leaks all over the hardwood floors, you're satisfied with the service and the insurance settlement.

So you go back to that agent when you buy a second property—this one a mountaintop loft where your family will weekend and vacation but never rent out. The up-front conversation is briefer this time, and the agent does her thing. You arrange payments through the mortgage company, and you even pay an initial bill for the first premium yourself. A year passes with no incident, and then the place burns down.

You call the company's claims hotline, and you're told you have no insurance. You call your insurance agent, who hasn't spoken to you in a year and has no recollection of your initial conversations. She says it's not her fault that you don't have insurance and you'd better not try to blame her. You call your mortgage company, which has no record of making this year's premium payment. You call your mother and cry on her shoulder.

Turns out the insurance agent assumed the mountain loft was a rental property, too, and wrote a policy that the underwriters canceled four months after it was issued, saying the company no longer insures rental properties in this mountaintop resort. A letter was sent to you at the address of the mountain property, which has no mail service, so you never received it. This is the first you've heard of the cancelation.

Whom will you hold accountable?

Before you answer that, consider whether that's the right question to ask. What's important here is not to assign blame, but to work something out with the insurance company so you can rebuild your beloved second home.

If you had to do it all over again, you might consider the quality of the "team" that's working on your behalf: the insurance agent, the underwriters, and the mortgage company. And you.

You are accountable for making sure your property is insured. Your property is not insured. You are accountable. Your insurance agent is accountable for writing the correct policy. She wrote the wrong policy, and it was canceled. She is accountable. The underwriters are accountable for notifying you of the cancelation. They sent the letter to an address without mail service and did not use certified mail. They broke no laws, and yet they failed to notify you. They are accountable.

The mortgage company did not set up payments because it never received a bill for the premium. Nobody from the bank checked in to ask you why, which would have brought the error to your attention. The bank, while it broke no laws, is accountable.

Yet nobody on the list is standing up and saying, "We're all accountable. Let's make it right." Instead, each one is blaming someone else. You're blaming the insurance agent. She's blaming underwriting. Underwriting is blaming you. Next time you buy insurance for another property, whom will you hold accountable for making sure your claim will be paid if it burns down?

You? You can't write the policy yourself. The agent? She isn't in charge of underwriting. The underwriters? They tried to notify you. The bank? It's not even in the insurance business. Even if just one of these parties is responsible, does that mean the others aren't?

Perhaps each of you is one-quarter responsible for making sure you have insurance. So if your place burns down, each of you can point only three-quarters of a finger at the others?

That's not going to work.

Try this on: Each person who touched that transaction is 100 percent responsible for making sure your place is insured. If you were 100 percent responsible, you would have followed up after the transaction with the agent and with the bank to verify that everything was in place. You also would have touched base with your agent periodically to make sure your insurance was adequate as you added furniture and electronics to the home.

If the agent were 100 percent responsible, she would have notified you of the cancelation herself instead of assuming you had received a letter from underwriting and had found alternative insurance. During the phone call, it's likely she would have discovered that you did not intend to rent out your place, and the policy would have been reinstated immediately.

If the underwriters were 100 percent responsible, they would have verified the address on the letter and, even though they are not required by law to send it via certified mail, they would have taken steps to verify that you received it. If they had done that, they would have known that you did not receive the letter and could have delivered the news about the canceled policy in another way.

If the mortgage company were 100 percent responsible, a representative would have let you know that the bank was not making the agreed-upon insurance payments because it had not received any "premium due" notices. That red flag likely would have led you to call the agent, and you would have known about the problem.

Next time you need insurance, how much responsibility do you want each person on your team to take for making sure you have it? Best guess: 100 percent.

Now flip the scenario. If you *sell* insurance, or financial planning, or bank services, or advertising—or anything—how responsible are you for making sure what you have sold is working out for the buyer? Do you leave it to the buyer to notify you if there's a problem? Do you assume the buyer will know there's a problem? The buyer might not have a clue.

You're the professional. You're the one who knows the ins and outs of your product. The accountable sales professional is 100 percent responsible for the customer's satisfaction—or in the case of the uninsured mountaintop homeowner, for the customer's protection. And if there's a problem, the accountable sales professional is the first one to say, "This is my responsibility as much as it is yours. Let's work together to solve the problem." That's teamwork.

THE CONTRADICTION

18

> " 'Circumstances beyond my control' doesn't
> mean you're not accountable. It means you don't
> understand teamwork. The team is accountable,
> and at the same time, the individual is
> accountable."
>
> —*Linda Galindo, accountability thought leader,*
> *speaker, coach, consultant, author*

True teamwork wasn't happening when Cecilia received a poor evaluation after her team leader, Grant, dropped the ball on their joint project. Neither Cecilia nor Grant had taken 100 percent responsibility for the success of that project before they started. That seems to contradict the theory that each member of a team is 100 percent accountable.

The fact is that although Cecilia and Grant had different roles, each had an equal amount of responsibility for the team's success. And each was 100 percent accountable for the team's outcome.

That the so-called "team" was not operating according to the high-accountability model doesn't mean 100 percent personal accountability wasn't an option for them. In fact, it is an option for every team member and every person. Accountability is a mindset. On a highly accountable team, every member has a mindset of 100 percent accountability.

A team that doesn't embrace 100 percent personal accountability is not a true team. It's a group of people working toward a common goal—and hoping everyone does his or her part. Good luck.

When Cecilia complains that she got a poor performance evaluation because another member of her team didn't get her what she needed when she needed it, it's clear that the team she is on isn't really a team at all. A real team includes the following:

- Clear roles.
- A clear goal.
- The expectation that you hold each other accountable and the authority to make good on it.
- Clear agreements that spell out who does what by when—with the understanding that any team member can renegotiate the commitment in advance of the deadline.
- The authority to let nonperformers go.
- The authority to add members to the team.
- The need and trust to depend on one another to get the job done.
- A team reward: If one of us fails, we all fail.

What a true team does *not* need is a manager. The team chooses a leader from among its members and then it self-manages.

When Cecilia asserts that the missed deadlines were not her fault and that she had no control or authority to force Grant to get her what she needed when she needed it, it's clear that Cecilia does not understand what personal accountability means. Fault, control, and authority have nothing to do with personal accountability. Personal accountability is about owning your results once you know how everything turns out, whether they are good or bad. That ownership must come without fault, blame, or guilt.

As a team member, Cecilia failed herself and her team by assigning blame instead of owning the result. If she had a mind-set of personal accountability before she started the project, she would have realized that *she* would own the outcome of the project, even though her team has multiple members, and even if one of them refuses to honor the agreed-upon deadlines.

She would have known she had to take action and risks to get what she needed from Grant, even if it meant speaking to the CEO, who is a personal friend of Grant's. She might have chosen to look for another team to join—a highly accountable team—even if it meant moving to a different company.

When you accept responsibility for whatever your outcomes will be before you agree to start a project, keep your lousy job, work for a CEO who doesn't hold everyone to the same standard, or join a team, you will either be much more clear about what you have to do so it all works out in your favor, or you will decide *not* to agree to it up front.

If you own the outcome of your actions *before* you know their results, you will stand out as a consistent, clarifying force in a world of inconsistent accountability.

HOW REAL IS YOUR TEAM?

Check off the following elements that are true of your team:

_____ Roles and authority are clear.

_____ The team goal is clear.

_____ The team definition of success for what the team owns is clear.

_____ We hold one another accountable and have the authority to make good on it.

_____ We operate with clear agreements that spell out who does what by when—with the understanding that any team member can renegotiate the commitment in advance of the deadline.

_____ The team has the ability and authority to let non-performers go.

_____ The team has the ability and authority to add members to the team.

_____ To get the job done and meet the customer's need, we must interdepend on one another and trust one another.

_____ There is a team reward: If one of us fails, we all fail.

If you checked none or only some of the statements, your group is not a true team.

19

FIVE LEVELS OF TEAMS

"In an ideal world, I would do what I'm doing now. In the past, it was just me and my boss, and we held each other accountable. Now I get to work with other people. There's more communicating, more energy. I like the dynamic."

—*Bryan Morrell, team leader*

For teamwork to work, all team members—and the executive to which the team reports—must know exactly what kind of team they're on. Calling a group a "team" doesn't make it a team. And within an organization, different kinds of teams might be needed for projects calling for different skills and results.

Introducing the team concept to an organization that traditionally has operated on the backs of people who prefer to work independently can be successful if you do it progressively, starting with traditional work groups and culminating with high-performing teams that are focused on results.

There are five levels of teams.

Level 1: The traditional work group. We call ourselves a team, but the "team" is simply a manager and everyone else. The manager assigns projects, directs group members, and manages in a traditional manner. Each team member reports to the manager, and anyone outside of the team communicates with team members through the manager. The manager alone evaluates each team member's performance and is accountable for the team's results.

Level 2: The manager-led group. Instead of independently creating goals and assignments, the manager of this group asks team members for input—and listens to it and acts on it. The manager guides the process of defining objectives, roles, job descriptions, and workflow, but the manager doesn't dictate these. Although the group has input, the manager retains final say. Group members report to the manager, and the manager is solely accountable for results.

Level 3: The self-managed team. This is where the culture change happens when it comes to teams. This is where accountability shifts from the manager to the team. On the self-managed team, the manager acts as team leader and facilitates clarification of roles, job descriptions, and work processes—but the team creates them. Decisions are made by consensus, and the team ensures that objectives are met. Team members, not the manager, evaluate each others' performance. A team member reports to the manager, and that role rotates as needed. The team—the whole team—is accountable for results.

Level 4: The self-directed team. This team selects its own leader, and the leadership role may rotate, depending on the project and which team member is most qualified to lead the effort. The team clarifies its own roles, job descriptions, and work processes; self-evaluates; and ensures that it achieves its objectives. A designated team member reports to the manager—who actually does very little managing of a team at this high level—and the team is accountable for the results.

Level 5: The high-performance team. This team doesn't need a manager to make assignments or figure out what's next. Members of a high-performance team know what they need to do day-to-day to achieve the team's goals, and they anticipate what's next and plan for it. No manager has to check on the team's progress, because it's evident that the team is progressing beyond expectations. This team consistently meets its goals, in part because the members evaluate their own and each others' performance. Anyone in the organization can approach any team member without asking for permission from the team's manager, who would tell the person, "Take it directly to Team Member A; he'll take care of it." The team leader reports to the manager, and the team is accountable for results.

A "group" becomes a "team" when the players hold each other accountable, without waiting for the manager to take action and without running to the manager to complain about disagreements and stalemates. Holding teammates accountable can be uncomfortable, especially if you've all become buddies and have not held each other accountable in the past.

Still, if you are committed to one another's success—and therefore to the success of your project, your team, and your company—you'll do the hard thing. You will talk *to* each other, not *about* each other. You will stop holding the "meeting after the meeting" so a few of you can secretly agree to a strategy different from those of others with whom you disagree. You do not gossip about teammates.

Instead, you will bring these issues to light with the "offending" teammate in the room. You will talk face-to-face. You will hold each other accountable, and you will be held accountable by the others on your team. You will solve any differences that way, and you will find solutions that way. That's teamwork.

Teams come together and break apart as needed, so team members work with lots of different colleagues on lots of different teams. "Once a team, always a team" is too static for a culture of teamwork. Team members who have the expertise needed for one project might be better matched with different co-workers on a different task.

And, sometimes, a team isn't needed at all. More companies are using "tiger teams" to solve specific problems. Once the problem is solved, the team members return to their independent producer roles until they are needed to solve the next problem.

TEAM LEVELS

Which level is your team?

Group Interaction	Level	Leadership	Reporting Structure
Manager assigns projects, directs group members, and manages in a traditional manner.	1	Traditional work group	Manager reports and is accountable for results.
Manager guides process of defining objectives, roles, job descriptions, and work flow. Group has input, but manager retains final say.	2	Manager-led group	Manager reports and is accountable for results.
Manager acts as team leader and facilitates clarification of roles, job descriptions, and work processes. Decisions are by consensus and team ensures objectives are met.	3	Self-managed team	A designated team member reports; reporting person changes as needed. Team is accountable for results.
Team selects leader; leader may rotate. Team clarifies roles, job descriptions and work processes, and ensures the achievement of objectives.	4	Self-directed team	A designated team member reports and is accountable for results.
Team selects leader. Team defines roles, job descriptions, and work processes. Team anticipates what is needed and decides how to do it. Team members evaluate one another's performance.	5	High-performance team	Team leader reports to manager. Team is accountable for results.

CHAPTER

20

ELEVEN BEHAVIORS

"Some people are more accountable than others; that's the dynamic of a team. When there's a problem, we all recognize that we're all guilty sometimes. So there's no punishment. Let's learn from the mistakes."

—*Bryan Morrell, team leader*

The same behaviors that characterize highly accountable individuals also make good team members and successful teams. Here are eleven behaviors that you can adopt as you work toward your mindset of 100 percent accountability as an independent sales professional or as a member of a team.

Talk to, Not About

The host of a long-running Midwestern radio talk show requires everyone on his ten-member team of advertising sales executives to attend a weekly, all-hands coaching session, with the hope that they will start sharing information, treating each other with respect, pulling together for the benefit of the show, and helping the company and one another succeed.

He's not seeing any progress, however. Two of the sales execs—a Type-A go-getter who consistently brings in business, and the host's down-to-earth brother, whose desire to treat clients as "partners" compels him to give away more free advertising than he sells—have never liked each other. Over time, they have formed alliances with other sales execs on the staff, and two camps have formed. Their workplace is stifled by animosity.

All week long, the sales execs slink into the host's office, close the door, and rant about their colleagues in the opposite camp. They complain about them, tattle on them, reveal personal information about them, and accuse them of wrongdoing.

The host is exhausted. So he issued a "talk to, not about" policy: If you want to talk to me about someone else on the staff, bring him or her along. Anything you're going to say to me about the person, you're going to say to him or her at the same time.

The policy didn't automatically eradicate gossip and pettiness from this workplace, but it drastically reduced the problem. As long as the leader was willing to listen to gossip, the staff felt free to engage in it. Now they don't have permission to gossip.

The boss also instructed the staffers to practice the "talk to, not about" strategy among themselves. Now, a sales executive who is approached by a colleague with gossip or complaints about someone else is more likely to say, "Let's go get Maryanne so she can hear this, too," or, "I am uncomfortable that the person you're talking about isn't here, so I'm not going to continue this conversation."

Take-away

Don't undermine your teammates or group leader by talking about them behind their backs. And actively help others to break the habit by refusing to listen to their gossip. Your team will function more as a unit than as a group of solo practitioners if you follow this advice.

Cancel the "Meeting After the Meeting"

Sandra rarely says a word during team meetings, even when she has a strong opinion for or against what someone else is proposing. But once the meeting is over, she can't shut up.

Sandra chooses the teammates with whom she will share her opinions—after the meeting is over. She quietly lobbies for what she wants, criticizes those who spoke at the meeting if she disagrees with them, and strikes deals with certain colleagues while leaving others out of the loop.

Her behavior is divisive. More than once, it has unraveled a consensus the team leader thought the group had struck, convinced a teammate to choose not to honor an agreement she made during a meeting, and slowed the team's progress on its project.

Take-away

Members of a true team conduct business out in the open. Instead of pushing a private agenda, present it to the group and try to get buy-in or at least a compromise that considers your point of view. Refuse to participate in a meeting-after-the-meeting; tell the instigator you'd like to invite the rest of the group.

Make Clear Agreements

The cornerstone of personal accountability, the clear agreement leads to good teamwork. Glenda, a real-estate agent, learned this when she took a job with a home builder to sell houses in a brand-new subdivision.

On her first day at work, Glenda agreed with the project's other two new real-estate agents that the three would evenly split their commissions so that each sales pro could spend one-third of her time outside of the sales office, working with the marketing director, following up with prospective customers, and completing post-sale paperwork. Because most of the sales would be to walk-in customers, two real-estate agents would staff the office at all times, leaving the third to work on marketing and paperwork. The three would rotate their schedules.

Glenda was happily working under that premise when a couple that had walked into the subdivision the prior weekend returned and asked for Roberta, who had worked with them on Saturday.

"Roberta isn't here today, but I can help you make your purchase," Glenda told the couple. They agreed, and after spending most of the day answering questions and evaluating the couple's finances, Glenda closed the sale.

In the meantime, another couple walked in, and the other real-estate agent on duty, Kathy, also made a sale.

Glenda was ecstatic over the success of the day. Split three ways, the combined $24,000 commission would pay each of the three women $8,000 for less than a day's work apiece. Roberta was delighted that her teammate had built on the foundation she had laid the prior weekend to make the sale.

Kathy was happier than anyone. She figured Glenda and Roberta had shared the work of the first sale and could split that commission. She was keeping the $12,000 from the sale she made on her own. "But we have an agreement to split all commissions three ways," Glenda reminded her.

"That's only when all three of us work on the same sale," Kathy challenged her.

"No; it's for every sale, no matter who touched it. That was our agreement."

"Show it to me," Kathy retorted.

Glenda never walked away from another meeting without a written agreement in her hands.

Take-away

Never assume that others at the table have the same understanding of an agreement as you do. Write down everything, from who will do which tasks, to the agreed-upon deadlines, to who gets the credit or the commission, and under what circumstances. Get everyone to agree to it, even if you trust your teammates. Do not say "yes" to anything before you fully understand what you're agreeing to—and until you are satisfied that everyone else on the team is on the same page.

Know Your Place

Kerry and Jimmy are new to sales and were hired by a large hotel chain to convince trade associations whose annual meetings are too small for a convention center to gather their members in the grand ballrooms of the company's hotels during low-traffic seasons.

Both highly motivated and highly accountable, the pair hit it off immediately. The two introduced themselves as a team to event planners at dozens of associations, kept each other up to date on every prospect so either one could handle calls from would-be clients if the other was unavailable, and shared the credit for their success when they reported to the sales manager that they had booked small conventions for three consecutive weekends in February.

"What do you mean you booked them?" a visibly annoyed sales manager asked the enthusiastic duo.

"We've got e-mail threads documenting their commitment to hold the meetings with us and our commitment to hosting them," beamed Jimmy. "All they need is a contract to sign. Just point us in the direction of legal, and we'll take care of that, too."

Turns out, team Jimmy and Kerry ranked pretty low on the chain of authority when it came to making commitments on behalf of the hotel giant. For that matter, so did the sales manager. The sales teams were supposed to find the leads, make the contacts, and get commitments—but not book specific dates. Dates were supposed to be cleared by the Reservations Department, the local hotel managers, and the legal staff before any contracts were drawn.

Oops.

Kerry and Jimmy meant well, worked hard, and did their job. But they overstepped their authority because they assumed they had more authority than they actually did. They would have saved a lot of back-pedaling if they had clarified that point with their boss.

Take-away

Before your team project begins, get clear about the role of the team and what the group is authorized to do, and about your specific role and your specific level of authority. Can you speak for the company? Can the team dismiss or add a member if everyone in the group agrees? Absolute clarity about roles, responsibilities, and limitations is key to a team's success.

Understand Priorities

Sometimes, the leaders to whom your team reports might disagree about their priorities—and your team's priorities.

Dennis's twelve-member research team has been so successful at supporting the sales professionals in the field without any slip-ups that he allows other managers and company executives to bring their suggestions, requests, and instructions directly to the team—without running them by him first.

The team has always figured out how to prioritize the requests and keep everyone happy, until a few weeks ago, when the vice president of sales approached one team member to ask him to start advising field representatives to back away from a new product. The next day, the vice president of marketing directed a different member to push the product so the field staff would sell more of it.

The team leader approached both VPs to ask for clarification and to point out the contradiction, and each one dug his heels in deeper. So the team leader brought the problem to Dennis for a resolution.

Highly accountable teams need little to no management. But when higher-ups are unclear about their priorities or contradict themselves or each other, and the direct approach—asking the one who has delivered the mixed messages for a clarification—doesn't clear up the confusion, superstar performers do what they need to do to get their work done.

Take-away

You can't be sure you're doing your work correctly if the leader who made the assignment isn't clear about what "correct" means. Contact and even confront the parties who need to know about the barrier to your team's success.

Learn from Your Mistakes

View the honest mistakes of others on your team as a chance for them to learn rather than as permission for you to punish them.

Molly dreaded admitting to the rest of her team that the big sale she was planning to close the day before fell through—and that meant her pals would not win the sales contest they thought they had all wrapped up. It turned out that the client, a friend of Molly's high-salaried aunt, couldn't afford to buy the high-end cookware her franchise sells, but she had not revealed that until Molly pressed her to sign on the dotted line. The young sales professional had not qualified the woman because she assumed she shared her aunt's income bracket and that her aunt wouldn't have introduced them if the woman were not a viable prospect. Plus, the woman had seemed delighted with the cookware ever since the aunt had shown off her own new set a few months earlier.

Popular with her teammates and a hard-working, if inexperienced, sales professional, Molly braced for an onslaught of finger-pointing from disappointed teammates who were counting on the contest's prize money. Instead, they playfully "booed" her, and then, one by one, they each revealed their most embarrassing, first-year-on-the-job *faux pas* to their young friend and colleague.

Then they talked to Molly about the importance of and techniques for qualifying prospects, and they came up with an unbeatable plan for winning next quarter's contest.

The accountable team member has no time for finding fault, placing blame, or even feeling guilty. Highly accountable people—and highly accountable teams—use their time identifying the problem and figuring out how to work together to solve it so they can get back to the task at hand.

When you look back at what went wrong, don't bother asking, "Whose fault was this?" or, if you're the likely culprit, "What is my punishment going to be?" Instead, admit your role and examine the following:

- This is what I did.
- This is what I learned.
- This is what I will do differently going forward.
- This is how I am accountable for what happened.
- This is my clear agreement for what I will do next. The agreement includes the consequences of breaking the agreement without appropriate, truthful, and timely renegotiation, given that circumstances can change.

Take-away

Accountability is a learning tool. Look back at your missteps, admit them, figure out how to avoid them next time, and move on.

Define "Success"

Individual sales professionals who have clearly defined success for themselves are more likely to achieve success than those who hope they will "recognize it if it happens." Likewise, the team whose members take the time to craft a definition of success for the group will be able to, together and as individuals, take the actions and risks that are necessary to be successful.

To Darryl, success is earning as much money every year as he can. To Latasha, success is making a positive difference in the world, especially when it comes to the environment.

So when the two teamed up to sell a mountain that belonged to the cash-strapped resort where they both work, they clashed so hard and so often that the resort manager took the job away from them—and they both forfeited the 1 percent commission they would have earned on the potential seven-figure sale.

Darryl set out to woo a developer who offered to pay top dollar, and who had planned to strip the mountain of its trees and convert the parcel into condominiums for skiers. Latasha spent her time trying to convince local nature foundations to pool their resources, buy the mountain, and preserve it in its natural state.

Both aimed to sell the mountain, but they never agreed how, to what kind of client, for how much, or whether the new owner's plan for the mountain would influence their choice of buyer. They never defined what "success" was for the team, opting instead to pursue each of their individual dreams.

In fact, they never were members of a true team. They were two people with the same ultimate goal—a sale—but no common definition of what success is.

Take-away

Success is rarely an accident. Come to a consensus on what "success" means for the team. Have this discussion with your teammates as a group. If you can't agree, consider repopulating the team with members who can agree on that critical foundation.

Don't Rescue, Fix, and Save

Michelle's teammate, Mike, can always count on her to bail him out. He routinely asks her to cover for him when he is running late, has personal business to take care of, or is about to miss a deadline. And she does.

Even when he doesn't ask for her help, Michelle frequently pitches in when she thinks the quality of Mike's work is lacking. She rescues, fixes, and saves her teammate. She figures it's better for her to cover for him, improve his work, and pick up his slack than for her team to get a bad reputation or for her friend to get in trouble with the boss.

So he takes advantage of her. She resents him for it, but she doesn't show it. She would rather continue rescuing, fixing, and saving than to have an uncomfortable conversation with a colleague about why he isn't honoring his commitments. She would rather do the extra work than hold her teammate accountable.

Yet by protecting him, she is punishing herself and her team's higher performing members, including some who don't know she is doing Mike's work. She—and they—deserve to work with an accountable colleague rather than someone who chooses to slack off. Her team would be stronger if she and the others held Mike accountable. She would be less stressed and more productive on her own if she stopped rescuing, fixing, and saving.

Take-away

When you don't hold underperformers accountable, you weaken the team. No amount of rescuing, fixing, and saving will make a team whole, because the offending member will never get stronger as long as you are propping him up.

Hold Yourself Accountable

Because nobody is holding Mike accountable, he figures there's no reason for him to hold himself accountable. Why work hard when someone else is willing to make it appear that you do?

Let's hope that's just a temporary strategy. In the long run, the only true way to succeed is honestly.

Your personal accountability depends on your willingness to own the outcomes of your behavior. Even though Mike is allowing someone to cover up his failures—and he's getting away with it, for now—he is still failing. He is not successful, plus he clearly does not have a mindset of accountability, which is critical to his success.

Take-away

How do you behave when nobody is looking? Are you accountable only when someone holds you accountable? Are you accountable only when you get caught? Highly accountable people own their behavior and the results of their behavior—good or bad, public or private. Hold yourself accountable so your teammates don't have to do it for you. They have better things to do.

Become "Conflict Competent"

Every night before she goes to sleep, Keesha prays for her teammates. She prays for Danny to stop bossing her around. She prays for Felicity to land a high-paying dream job—far, far away from anyplace Keesha will ever work. She prays for her team leader, Brenda, to get a clue.

Keesha does not like working with her teammates. Their personalities clash with hers and they clash with one another. She doesn't respect their work styles. She is intimidated by those who are loud and dominate team meetings, and she thinks her team leader is incompetent. So she prays and prays.

What might be quicker is a conversation with each team member, in which she addresses her problems with each of them. What might be more effective is for her to talk to her teammates about how they can work together for the success of the team and for one another's peace of mind.

But Keesha is not conflict competent, so she does not talk to anyone about the problems these personality clashes create for the team and what it produces. She avoids conflict. She lets it go when someone refuses to embrace a mindset of accountability to the detriment of the team or to herself. She hopes other teammates will have those conversations with the offending colleagues or that someone from human resources will ride in on a white horse to rescue, fix, and save her.

So far, her prayers remain unanswered. In the meantime, Keesha could educate herself about how to confront a teammate productively about his or her behavior and how to have conversations that result in healing and improvement rather than shouting and hard feelings.

Take-away

On a team whose members are 100 percent accountable for the success of the group, everyone must be willing to truthfully and respectfully confront a member who is causing a problem for an individual or for the team. And there's no need to go it alone. Plenty of primers about conflict resolution and about having tough conversations are on the bookshelves, and every human resources department has managers who can coach associates in the art of solving team problems.

Work Transparently

Steve stays at the office later than anyone else on his team, almost every evening. He files all of the day's paperwork before he leaves for the night, reads all of the newspaper business sections to keep up with trends and new regulations, searches the Web for sales tips, and makes two to-do lists every day: one for the day's activity and the other for his obligations to each case or client. He makes lists of the prospects he will call and reviews the detailed notes he took during each phone conversation from the prior day.

Everyone knows Steve puts in long hours. Yet at the end of the week, he routinely comes up short on closed sales and drags down the team's collective numbers.

Keeping busy and staying at work until the wee hours doesn't make Steve productive. His activity isn't translating into sales because it's not the kind of activity that sells. It's the kind of activity that makes him look busy.

Don't make busywork for yourself. Hold yourself accountable by allowing others on your team to see and know exactly what you are working on. Avoid talking about how busy you are. Talk instead about how great your results are.

Take-away

Numbers tell the story in sales. Show your teammates and your bosses your numbers, not the number of hours you work.

ARE YOU A TEAM PLAYER?

Rate yourself on each characteristic of a high-performing team member. Scale: 1 = Poor, 5 = Excellent

_____ Talk to, not about, others.

_____ Attend no "meetings after the meetings."

_____ Make clear agreements.

_____ Set a clear goal.

_____ Establish a clear definition of success.

_____ Set clear roles.

_____ Understand authority.

_____ Establish a clear decision-making process.

_____ Do not "rescue, fix, and save."

_____ Hold yourself and others accountable.

_____ Be conflict competent.

_____ Be transparent.

CHAPTER

BARRIERS 21 TEAMWORK

> "Understand which of the activities you do produce
> revenue and which activities are busywork. The
> biggest challenge in our business, because
> there's so much to do, is understanding what the
> revenue activities are. Hone your skill set in
> those activities."
>
> —*Ann Swartz, chief operating officer*

Too often, an organization, its executives, and its culture create barriers to true teamwork. The usual culprit: their definition of "team."

"Welcome to our team." That requires some clarification.

Here are a few good questions to help you get clear on the concept:

- What kind of team is your team?
- Do I have to work as part of a team if I work for you?
- Is there any room for solo acts?
- For the financial planner who prefers to work independently and has a successful track record of stellar results without a team, is working on a team an option? A suggestion? A non-negotiable?

When companies convince their superstar earners to join teams when they don't want to, two consequences can result:

- Most will continue to operate as individuals, except they'll assign themselves the role of team leader and bark orders to their teammates so everyone does things the way the leader wants. Those producers will ignore input and objections from their teammates. You can call that a team, but giving it that label doesn't make it a team.

- Some will form alliances with a specific team member or two and promise to reward them on the sly for meeting the demands that will allow the producer to continue to operate independently. Maybe the superstar will share information with these hand-picked assistants but not with the rest of the team, or enlist their help for unpleasant tasks such as taking emergency calls from clients in the middle of the night. That's profitable for those "special" team members, but it's not so great for the team. "One for all and all for one" doesn't work when "one" is making all the decisions and "all" aren't even aware of what those decisions are.

If you are the manager who assigned the team, you've got a challenge: to get the top earners to buy into teamwork and to consider their own success the team's success—and vice versa. That means the top earner must consider every team member's contribution to be as important as his or her own.

If you are the leader of a sales force, you might empathize with your team-averse mega-producers because you, too, found success as an independent operator. But if you have determined that working on teams will make your top producers even more successful and your company more profitable, and if you have decided to make teamwork mandatory, then it's up to you to hold these producers accountable for being good members of the team.

Consider the team mentality of basketball great Larry Bird, who most sports fans would agree was the Boston Celtics' most valuable player for most of his thirteen years with the team. You might remember that this front-court legend didn't thump his chest or sing his own praises nearly as often as he could have. He was a superstar, yet he acknowledged that if every player on the team performed his best, all of them would shine brighter and win more games.

Contrast that with the unstoppable Michael Jordan, whom fans of the Chicago Bulls identified as the heart of the team and who played as if he were the only one on the court. Considered the greatest basketball player ever, nobody can dispute his enormous talent and enduring success or imagine that he could be any better as a player. Yet he could have been a better team member and leader, especially during his early years on the team. It wasn't until this domineering player learned to trust his teammates and his coach that the team started to win NBA titles. With that change, Jordan became a true leader—the kind who makes his teammates, and his team, better.

Like lone-dog sales professionals who believe they *are* the team, Jordan didn't rely on his team members as much as he could have. The person who is "the one" on a team very often has a hard time seeing that he would be more successful if he embraced the support of his teammates and allowed their talents to shine as well.

It's understandable: Because they are so successful on their own, superstars have evidence they're doing everything right. Why should they do it differently when what they're already doing works? That's a question for the leader of the sales force to tackle: Seriously, why *should* they do it differently?

The answer might be that some shouldn't.

Many companies successfully embrace a culture that fosters an environment in which sales professionals thrive independently, reap individual successes and profits, and reach out for help and resources whenever they need to—without throwing in with a specific group. Others have moved to a culture of teamwork and insist that sales professionals work on teams with other sales professionals, managers, researchers, and assistants, because industry trends point to higher profits and happier endings through the team model.

What those diverse cultures must have in common to succeed is *informed consent*. If you hire a sales professional with the promise of a supportive, accountable team, make good on that. If your culture supports individuals who work on their own, say so. You'll have nothing but trouble with a recruit who accepts your offer of a job as an independent producer if the new associate learns after the fact that you expect him or her to work enthusiastically as part of a team.

Be clear and honest about what you expect, up front. Allow your recruit to say either, "I can agree to that" or, "This isn't for me. I'll work somewhere else." Then, hold that new associate accountable for that choice, for doing what he or she signed on for.

If you're serious about creating and maintaining a team culture, pin part of each sales professional's commission to achieving team goals. Ask team members to evaluate one another's performance rather than doing it yourself. Learn whether each member has a mindset of 100 percent accountability for the team's success—not only for his or her small part in it.

Likewise, for individuals who sign on to work independently, don't accept excuses and blame when the lone wolf falls short of goals and points the finger at you or the support staff for not pitching in enough. Hold the independent producer accountable for taking the necessary actions and risks—including asking for help.

Moving in this direction—from a culture of independent producers to a culture of teamwork—takes time. Any change takes time to become successful. You can't force individual producers who are making money hand over fist to embrace teamwork. You can hope for it, but you can't force it.

What you can do is take the time to make the culture change gradually. You can open a division of your organization that uses the team model and recruit new sales professionals into that division. Those professionals will accept their jobs knowing they are expected to work in teams. Or you can start creating small teams to work with specific products, and ask those teams to come up with business plans that can be accomplished only by a team.

Going forward, your organization might recruit more heavily for team players. This is a strategic decision: Will your company continue to thrive by relying on independent producers, or is teamwork important to the success of your sales-oriented business? A company that has traditionally embraced the independent producer can continue to do so, even as it incorporates teams into the culture.

The fact is that many sales professionals prefer to work on their own. Others are more comfortable and productive as part of a team. The two work styles can co-exist. That can work as long as the sales professionals you hire know which role you expect them to fill: independent producer or team member. You need to decide whether new recruits have a choice, or if you will assign them to work alone or as part of a team. If you give a job candidate that information before offering a job, the recruit can make an accountable choice.

Hiring newcomers who want and expect to work as part of a team but then changing the game once they're onboard—so they're expected to work independently—is not likely to reap the results you want. Likewise, forcing someone who signed on as an independent producer to join a team probably won't work out in favor of either the company or the associate. Be clear and upfront about how you will require each new hire to work. The fewer surprises your associates encounter when they come on board, the fewer disappointments for them and for you when you tally results.

CHAPTER

22

REASONABLE EXPECTATIONS

"Accountability has to be reasonable; expectations
need to be doable."

—*Bryan Morrell, team leader*

Team leader Charlie wants the eight members of his team to be accountable as individuals *and* as a team. Here is how he encourages that.

Team members are allowed to say "no" to him and to each other if they are asked for help but are too busy with their own tasks to pitch in—as long as they explain why. "In the long run, it's easier for me if they give me an honest 'no' than if they say 'yes' and then complain after the fact," he says.

Everyone on the team knows how productive every teammate is each week. Charlie shows them how many client proposals and financial plans each person completed the prior week. Someone who has especially low numbers can explain why. That often helps others understand that the low producer was working on an especially difficult case or had a couple of slow days while learning about a new product. Sometimes, the others offer to pick up the slack until the low producer is back on track.

The team also knows how well the firm does every week. This sales team supports the financial advisors, so Charlie shows the team how the advisors performed during the week as well, and he makes the connection between the team's high or low numbers and the advisors' high or low numbers.

Colleagues cover for one another during vacations to keep the work flow consistent. Occasionally, taking on the extra work load will help a team member shine. One woman on the team, for instance, consistently cranked out thirty proposals a week—a respectable outflow. When a teammate was out for a week, she took on her colleague's work and wound up doubling her output. Once she knew what she was capable of, she continued to finish sixty proposals a week.

Charlie doesn't tolerate finger-pointing when there's a problem. "With accountability," he says, "we don't blame people. We take ownership of the problems." Fault, says the team leader, is "a negative thing. You never get a good response when you approach someone with negativity." His approach: "Let's move to what the solution is."

If a team member neglects to follow up with an advisor, Charlie's public response is that the sales desk made the mistake, so the team, and not one individual, takes the hit. The team privately identifies the offending member, works on a solution, and creates an internal plan to prevent the same problem from occurring again.

The team leader knows the personal goals of every member of the team. If someone seems frustrated with the work, he asks what the person would rather be doing. If the person's goal is to move to another area of the company, Charlie tries to make that happen. "In most cases, nobody has ever asked them what they want," he notes. "They appreciate it."

Charlie's philosophy is, "Accountability has to be reasonable; expectations need to be doable." When the CEO mandated that the team fill every advisor's request within two hours of receiving it, the young manager stepped up for his team. "When you're getting eight to twelve e-mails an hour, that expectation is too high. Two hours might be a quick answer, but it's not the right answer." His resolution: The sales desk calls each advisor within a few minutes of receiving the request to gauge the urgency of the job and estimate the time in which it will be completed.

The manager spends some social time with the team. While Charlie won't "get crazy" with his staff, he believes that bonding outside of work helps build relationships at work. When one team member scored a half-dozen Red Sox tickets for an afternoon game, for instance, Charlie allowed a group to go. He helped select the lucky fans, and included one team member who had recently passed a difficult licensing exam and another who had higher-than-average productivity the week before.

Charlie's behavior is the example for the team. He arrives at work by 7 A.M. every day and leaves by 6 P.M. He doesn't come to work tired. He doesn't goof off during the day. "I can't ask others to work harder if I'm not doing it myself," he says.

Part III

ACCOUNTABILITY
AND LEADERSHIP

THE ACCOUNTABLE LEADER

23

> "The more personally accountable you are, the
> fewer checks and balances you need."
> —*Chris Litterio, managing partner*

Charlie has barely begun what is sure to be a very short climb to the C-suite of his company. The young manager knows something many seasoned supervisors, executives, and even CEOs haven't figured out yet: There's no need to train associates to be accountable.

The leader who embraces a mindset of personal accountability teaches it by example. To encourage and even ensure accountability in others, business leaders must be accountable themselves. The culture of an organization flows down from the top. If leaders at a company's highest level model personal accountability, it is far more likely to be a priority for the staff than if the bosses do not have the mindset.

A leader with a mindset of 100 percent personal accountability is a courageous person. Whether something goes wrong or right, the accountable leader stands in the same light. This leader is accountable for the results of his actions and for the actions of those who work for him, whether they turn out to be good or bad, right or wrong, popular or vilified.

The CEO who publicly states he is not responsible for the behaviors, actions, and outcomes of the executives who work for him is setting an example for his associates to follow. That CEO is inviting lower-level managers to throw up their hands and say, "Not my fault!" when their own subordinates make shady deals in the name of the company.

Accountability in an organization begins with the leader who refuses to make excuses, assign blame, or renege on agreements. Accountability in a corporate culture begins with a leader who makes every expectation perfectly clear.

Accountable leaders typically are at the helm of accountable organizations. Accountable organizations typically experience the following:

- Retention rates go up. Associates thrive in an environment of accountability because it's creative, it encourages problem-solving, and it is often lean—in the positive sense—because people are focused on results and not on busywork and because less-accountable associates weed themselves out.

- Communication is rampant. It might seem counterintuitive that a highly accountable organization would be less restrictive than an organization whose leader does not have the mindset. But an accountable environment encourages creativity, collaboration, teamwork, and honesty. So people are not afraid to speak their minds, share their ideas, and admit their mistakes.

- Production improves. Highly accountable sales professionals in a highly accountable workplace spend their time on the activity that results in sales: calling prospects, taking meetings, closing sales. They don't spend their time blaming each other or defending themselves when others blame them, because nobody looks for fault, blame, or guilt when something goes wrong. In fact, in a culture where accountability is expected and appreciated, the focus is sharply on money-making tasks.

- Compliance issues evaporate. The more accountable a company, its leader, and its associates, the less often they deal with compliance breaches.

The personal accountability of an organization's leader is the foundation of the organization.

How solid is your company's foundation?

CHAPTER

PAIN POINT: RETENTION

The annual staff turnover rate of financial advisors industry-wide is about 89 percent. That means only 11 percent of the people who become advisors for investment companies keep their jobs for more than a year. During four years at Baystate Financial, average turnover was 27 percent. That means 73 percent of the new advisors stayed on the job. Despite their better-than-average turnover rates, the question Baystate's leaders grapple with during meetings is this: What happened to that 27 percent?

What's the difference between Baystate and competitors that lose advisors faster than they can replace them? At Baystate, managers are accountable for recruiting and hiring people—between fifteen and twenty-five recruits a year—who are a good fit for the company and the job, and they are accountable for recognizing that not everybody is a good fit. Also, Baystate executives are accountable for setting hiring goals that are achievable and reasonable.

Baystate knows that low retention is a symptom of poor hiring. So the managers tasked with recruiting and hiring are as accountable for retention as the managers whose advisors up and quit within a year or two.

A financial services/investment company that forces its managers to hire thirty-plus advisors a year is setting itself up for continued high turnover; yet many, many do this year after year.

In the absence of a quality recruiting plan, those managers can't possibly hire that many qualified people. So they hire anyone— and sometimes everyone—who fills out an application.

That perpetuates an awful cycle of hiring badly, dealing with poor performance, terminating those who aren't working out, blaming the recruiters, and then giving them an even bigger goal for the next year. Eventually, the hiring managers get fired, too, and are replaced with new managers who won't be able to fulfill an unreasonable headcount quota any better than those who got the boot.

Want to stop the cycle? Stop hiring anybody and everybody. Stop buying into the fallacy that any warm body is better than no body at all. It's not true.

Be accountable for hiring "keepers." Be accountable for hiring advisors whom you are proud to introduce to your clients and whom you trust with their financial futures. Be accountable for hiring the kind of people you would trust with your own investments. Be accountable for changing the way your organization hires from an "event" to a "process."

An event looks like this: "Hello, I love you, and you're great. Let's get the paperwork started." A process looks like this: "Bring me your client files. Let's make sure the way you work with your clients is the way we want you to work with our clients. Share the names of three to five of your existing clients so I can call them for references."

Be accountable for setting the bar higher when it comes to vetting job candidates and offering positions. Be accountable for changing the goal from *hiring* as many people as you can to *retaining* them all.

Start by turning the interview into a process that involves multiple meetings and tough realities. Here is a ten-point checklist that can help:

1. Dig deep into the person's background during the interviewing and reference-checking process. Ask questions of the

applicant, his or her existing clients, and former employers or colleagues that reveal the candidate's level of integrity, competency, professionalism, and work ethic.

2. Ask pointed questions that will allow the candidate to reveal how dedicated he or she is to personal success and to the success of the company. For example, you might ask, "How are you going to feel about driving to a client meeting when it's snowing?"

3. Gauge the applicant's grasp of the reality of your business. For someone applying for a job in sales or as a financial advisor, for instance, you might ask, "Do you understand that you will spend 80 percent of every day during your first three years in this job going to appointments or setting up appointments?"

4. Get to know the candidate. Meet with the applicant and his or her spouse over dinner with you and your own spouse. Talk about sports, kids, and politics. Let your hair down. Laugh. Get to know the candidate as a person, not just as a businessperson.

5. Invite the candidate's spouse to ask questions. Gauge his or her understanding and attitude about the position, the hours, the travel, working on commission, and the potential sacrifices that are required for success, especially during the first few years on the job.

6. Involve the firm's higher-ups to meet the candidate. Offer a job only after the candidate has impressed a couple of other successful advisors and executives at the company. If the applicant is new to the business, the highest executives can meet the candidate after the recruiting manager has already decided to hire. If the person is a successful industry vet, get the C-suite involved right away.

7. Schedule six to eight interviews with executives before hiring a newcomer to the field, and five to seven for an

experienced financial professional. Stretch the process out over six to eight weeks, so both your offer and the candidate's response are thoughtful and based on lots of facts and insight.

8. Favor candidates who are successful in good jobs with other companies. Someone who is willing to leave a well-paying job to work for you obviously sees great value in joining your organization. A well-employed candidate is more likely to accept the job on its merits than a job-hunter who is desperate to get out of an unhappy situation.

9. Make it your goal not only to hire the candidate, but to retain the candidate. Gauge the applicant's commitment, long-term plans, desires for lifestyle and income, and expectations. The more you know about what the applicant wants, the better you can determine whether a job at your company will help him or her get it.

10. Go out of your way to recruit an especially good candidate. Managers at Baystate will drive from Boston to Vermont, or even farther, to meet with a successful financial advisor who has expressed an interest in joining the firm. If you know that adding someone to your organization will be good for your firm's culture and its bottom line, do what you have to do to make the interview happen.

BARRIERS TO ENTRY

Along the way, satisfy yourself that the applicant can both handle the job and perform it as you and your organization see fit. Don't just take the candidate's word for it. Require each promising potential new hire to *show* you what he or she is capable of by making some tough decisions and by completing an assignment that proves the candidate is serious about the job and competent to do it.

Baystate Financial Services, for example, requires inexperienced candidates to choose a specialty market to focus on: doctors, college professors, or accountants, for instance. Then each candidate is asked to conduct fifty marketing surveys of potential clients in that market during the next several weeks. An experienced applicant is asked to survey fifteen to twenty-five clients in his or her own market.

The surveys include fifteen to twenty questions similar to the following:

- Do you already have a financial advisor?
- What do you like or dislike about the advisor?
- Would you recommend this advisor to others?

That's a big assignment, and not everyone will do it. Some will freeze or freak out, and that's OK. This business isn't for everyone, and realizing the job isn't a fit before it starts is better than hiring someone who isn't up for it. Others will say they're offended that they have to prove themselves before being hired.

That's what happened when a star player for the New England Patriots applied for a job as a financial advisor at Baystate. He figured clients would flock to him because of his fame. He refused to conduct the fifty surveys and, in fact, withdrew his application when he learned about the prehire assignment.

He wound up getting a job with a competitor, and he quit that job within a few months. He failed because he waited for clients to find him instead of reaching out to them. If he had done the fifty surveys required by the recruiter, he would have realized before he accepted a job that it wasn't right for him.

A similar survey exercise can show the employer whether job candidates have what it takes to work in a position that requires reaching out to strangers and asking for business. And it can show applicants not only whether the job is a good fit, but whether their focus is viable.

One twenty-six-year-old frustrated schoolteacher who applied for a job as a financial advisor chose young schoolteachers as her market. During her surveys, she realized that the lifestyle and income of young schoolteachers limited the amount of money they could invest and the amount of insurance they needed and could afford. So the exercise made the schoolteacher-turned-advisor more aware of how difficult it would be to build a successful career as a financial advisor to that market. And she decided to rethink her career change.

Another young recruit opted out when he learned that the CEO was going to listen in as the applicant placed ten phone calls to potential clients. The exercise was designed to allow the executive to hear how the candidate dealt with people and whether he could perform well under the pressure of having the boss on the line. He couldn't.

You might be thinking that Baystate creates barriers to entry for would-be financial advisors. And you would be correct. Baystate recruiters are accountable for maintaining the firm's low turnover rate. The more barriers to entry they create, the better the chance that they will find the best people—those who have what it takes to earn and enjoy long-term success in the field.

Still, Baystate has a "recruiting reservoir" of nearly forty qualified potential new hires. These are people the CEO, the recruiters, or other executives have met and believe would be a good fit for the organization. All are successful in similar jobs at other organizations. Every quarter, the CEO reaches out to everyone on the list. He occasionally invites them to join a group of advisors at a ballgame or a seminar. He sends them the company newsletter. He lets them know he's ready to talk when they're ready to change jobs.

He doesn't leave hiring to chance, so he doesn't hire in a panic.

CHAPTER

26

CULTURE CLASH

A focus on accountability is critical if you're growing your company by buying small businesses and taking on their associates.

Answer two questions before you bring the office on board:

- Is it more important to acquire associates who will follow your firm's formula for success—whether that means making forty calls a day or forty sales a quarter—or to bring in companies whose associates have adopted a mindset of 100 percent accountability?
- Does the small business you're interested in operate in a culture that expects, encourages, and rewards highly accountable behavior?

If you absorb a business whose associates are willing to be accountable 65 percent of the time or for 65 percent of their outcomes, will that culture clash with your expectation that associates be 85 percent accountable? Or 100 percent accountable?

HIRING INTEGRITY

Baystate Financial operates under four principles: integrity, competence, professionalism, and work ethic. When the firm's recruiters interview job applicants, they look for candidates with those four qualities.

Competence and work ethic are difficult to determine from an interview, so a recruiter gauges those principles by asking the candidate's references whether the potential associate possesses those qualities. But integrity and professionalism often are obvious on first impression.

When a Baystate marketing director arrived in the company's lobby to greet a young woman who was interviewing for an entry-level position, the director found the candidate engrossed in the screen of her BlackBerry. "Just a sec," the candidate told her would-be boss. "I'm in the middle of a message." The marketing director interviewed the young woman but did not hire her. And she told her why. Another company might hire her, but not Baystate. Says the marketing director: "If I took her to an industry meeting and she acted like that, my peers would say, 'You've got to be kidding.'"

Baystate won't hire someone who shows up for an interview dressed like it's Saturday. Or a candidate who's chewing gum, or one who's late. A manager who ignores blatant symptoms of an unprofessional attitude is accountable for that new hire's predictably *laissez-faire* behavior on the job. If your expectation is that associates will put business before personal matters while at work; will respect the presence of another person in the room and engage with him or her, even when a text message from a friend is waiting; will dress professionally to meet colleagues, bosses, and clients; and will show up on time and ready to work, then hire people who declare those intentions with their actions, demeanor, and appearance during the job interview.

Someone who brushes off the greeting of a potential employer by telling her to "wait a minute" while she attends to personal business either does not intend to land that job or doesn't care one way or the other.

Is that the new associate you want to work for you? If it is, that's great. Hire her and tolerate her casual attitude. And you *will* have to tolerate it, because that's the attitude you are choosing by hiring her. That's the attitude you are condoning. That's the attitude you are inviting her to bring to work with her every morning. You are accountable for her behavior as much as she is if you endorse it with a job offer. Don't expect her to shape up once you tell her later that she can't act that way at work. You've already told her she can. She accepted the job with the expectation that she can. That's on you.

If she is not the kind of associate you want, however, send her packing—even if you're desperate to fill the position. The choice you make the day you hire someone can translate into problems or profits. Your hiring choice makes you accountable for whichever one results.

Here are two questions whose answers can reveal a job candidate's level of integrity:

- When in your life have you made a decision that you're proud of—when nobody was looking?
- Which five adjectives best describe your character?

One would-be associate, Leonard, replied to the first question by recounting the time he found a camera on the backseat of a taxi in Boston. He showed it to the driver, who said he was going to keep the camera. Leonard refused to give it to him, but not because he wanted to keep it for himself. Instead, he turned it into the cab company's lost and found, which later returned the camera to its owner.

That's the kind of story Baystate Financial's managers like to hear during job interviews. It's the kind of story that reveals the level of a job candidate's integrity.

If it's important to you to hire associates with integrity, ask them about it during the job interview. Integrity can be learned, or it can be innate. Either way, you can find out if it's part of an applicant's nature before you offer a job.

If Leonard had answered that question by saying, "I'm not sure; I've got to think about it," he probably would not be a financial advisor with the firm right now.

People with integrity can point to any number of experiences that reveal their true characters. Someone might recall not cheating on a test in college, even though it would have been easy to get away with it. Another might tell about returning an overpayment to a customer who never would have known she had paid the wrong amount. This question calls for a thoughtful answer; it's a question that a person with integrity can answer with ease.

When you ask for adjectives, listen carefully for words that reveal how much the candidate cares about other people and about doing the right thing: *honest, respectful, punctual, curious, accountable*. Beware of adjectives that indicate an "all-about-me" mindset: *carefree, fun, laid back*. Those qualities are great, however, when balanced by responsible and professional behaviors. Quiz your candidates to find out who they are.

CHAPTER

TRIANGLE OF VICTIMIZATION

28

Once you're satisfied that your recruit is honest, hard-working, outgoing enough to talk to strangers and ask for a sale, committed to working for your company, and has a mindset of personal accountability, you've only just begun. You'll need to manage your own expectations of even the most promising young talent you recruit into your firm.

The key is to start slow. Make your expectations clear, and make them reasonable. A new associate can be overwhelmed during the first few days at a new job. Give him or her an opportunity to start with a small project that offers a good chance for success. That small win will give the associate a chance to start off right. It will allow him or her to begin thinking, "I can do this job. I can be successful here."

Throwing a huge chore at a newcomer right away can yield the opposite result. Asking a new hire to make forty phone calls on his or her first day at a new job can seem like an insurmountable task. Scale it back. Ask for twenty. Then ask, "How do you feel about making twenty phone calls today?" Once your newbie succeeds, check in again: "How do you feel about the success of the day? Are you ready to ramp it up tomorrow?" You'll both feel good about the associate's first day.

If you dump too much on someone who's new and learning, you're setting up your prized new associate for failure. When the newbie fails, he or she will disappoint you.

It's a triangle of victimization. You expect too much of me. I fail. You're disappointed because I failed. You make us both victims.

Increase your expectations gradually to give the new hire time to adjust and develop a level of confidence. It all starts with baby steps.

Of course, you have to set benchmarks for your sales staff. You have to dictate quotas. You have to ensure they make their numbers so the company can meet its financial goals. But make those expectations reasonable. Ensure that they are doable. Don't expect a newbie to pull down huge commissions during the first year. Start slow, and allow the associate to rise to his or her potential without rushing. Allow—and expect—the new associate to move the needle forward a little bit every day. Make it OK if he or she has an occasional off day.

If you have recruited well and hired wisely, this accountable associate will meet and exceed your expectations and stay with your company for many years. That's if you don't scare the person away with too much too soon. And if the associate does his or her part. Occasionally, it doesn't work out, no matter how carefully you have vetted an applicant. And if you have been careful, it can be difficult to figure out why a new associate didn't work out.

The fact is, the sales professionals who earn at the bottom 10 percent of an organization have access to the same resources as those in the top 10 percent. The difference, most often, is that the top professionals have a mindset of accountability, and the others do not.

You can, however, approach those at the bottom of the earnings heap and ask them, "How can I help you earn more?" You can coach them, offer them more resources, and give them another chance to shine. People who do not embrace a mindset of personal accountability probably will not respond to your efforts. They don't want anyone to pressure them to perform, to succeed, or even to earn more money. And, sometimes, you just have to say, "I like you, but it's not working out for either of us. It's time for you to go."

CHAPTER

29

UNDERSTANDING THE GAME

A firm with a high retention rate of sales professionals almost certainly makes the demands of the job perfectly clear to every recruit. Nobody changes the game once a new associate comes on board. Job candidates need to understand what the game is—what is expected of them once they sign on.

They want to know answers to the following questions.

How much of my income is salary versus commission?

A typical practice at brokerage houses or small, hybrid organizations that both sell insurance and provide financial planning services is to pay financial advisors a small salary plus commission for the first three years. After three years, it's all commission.

How am I expected to earn these commissions? Can I figure that out on my own, or does the company have a process that everyone must follow?

The answers depend on the culture of your organization. Some CEOs dictate that sales professionals make a certain number of phone calls a day and close a specific quantity of sales each month or quarter. Those CEOs require associates to keep track of their activity and provide a "scorecard" every Friday that details the week's calls, meetings, and sales. Other CEOs skip the scorecard and allow the sales professionals to hit the numbers in whichever way works for them. Either way, sales professionals have to make their numbers. Reveal those numbers to potential recruits so they can make an informed decision about whether to join your firm—and give informed consent when they agree to take on a job that requires what you require.

How much of a commission will I earn on each sale, and what is the "split" with the company?

Depending on what you are selling, of course, the range of commissions varies. Lay this out for your recruits so they know exactly which products pay what amount. That way, they can decide whether they want to specialize, for example, in selling life insurance, which pays them the most, or another product, which might be easier to sell but provides less of a return to the seller.

How much does an average producer at your firm earn each year?

The answer is different at every firm. Best practice: Reveal to job candidates how much they can expect to earn in salaries and commissions during their first three years with your company, and when salaries will stop and commission-only income will kick in. Let them know how much a typical advisor earns per year after Year Three.

How flexible are you when it comes to work hours and face time in the office?

This is an important question, because for some, arriving at 8 A.M. and sitting at a desk all day will cramp their selling style. Many sales professionals consider themselves entrepreneurs, even when they are employed by an organization, and they like to work out of their cars, meet clients after hours, or spend time cultivating relationships with clients on the golf course. Others might be more comfortable connecting with prospects via Facebook or LinkedIn than on the telephone.

If you fail to make it clear to a potential associate that her manager will lock her out of her office if she's not there by 8 A.M., so she has to find her supervisor and explain her tardiness, you're not going to retain that associate once that happens. On the other hand, someone who thrives in a culture of structure and across-the-board rules isn't going to devote too many months to an organization that is so casual that it seems to enforce no policies at all. You'll have a better chance of retaining a financial advisor who joins your organization with informed consent—that is, she understands your company's culture before she chooses to accept the job, and she buys into it, knows it suits her style, and willingly agrees to abide by it.

Still, recruiters too often fudge their answers to those questions so they can fill vacancies in an organization—even if it means they're adding staffers for whom the culture isn't a fit. Recruiters and sales managers are under pressure to find and train recruits, to go into the field to help each new hire build a business, to manage the sales process, and to make sure the paperwork gets done.

How much can one person do? The accountable leader realizes that forcing associates to overcommit is like pouring water into an empty cup but not stopping when the water starts spilling all over the table. It's like forcing someone who's thirsty to drink out of a fire hose. She won't drink much water and will walk away with a sore face.

CHAPTER 30

PAIN POINT: HOLDING OTHERS ACCOUNTABLE—OR NOT

Eve had a rough couple of years, and her manager, Teresa, really felt for her. Within a twenty-month stretch, Eve's daughter had been diagnosed with a heart condition, her father had died after a long illness, her husband left her, and a tree crashed through the roof of her home during a bad storm.

Understandably, she took some family medical leave to help her daughter and her father before he passed away. After working in a supporting role at the company for half a dozen years, nobody would begrudge her the time off she needed. But when she returned to work, she wound up in arguments with the sales professionals she was supposed to be helping, started strolling in to work later and later, and routinely left early and took too much unscheduled time off.

So when a promotion that Eve wanted came up, Teresa bumped someone else up into the job. Eve responded by gossiping about Jen, her colleague who got the promotion even though Jen had fewer years of experience than Eve. Eve undermined Jen every chance she got by lying about her. She also continued calling in sick and coming in late. And a few times, when colleagues needed to track Eve down on sick days, they learned she was moving, visiting relatives, or even shopping.

Still, Teresa kept her on board, figuring she was going through a rough patch and the last thing she needed was to be reprimanded. It turned out that Teresa—an executive-level department head—was the one who got reprimanded, however. Her boss told her she wasn't being a good business partner to Jen because she was allowing Eve to spread rumors and undermine her. And he told her she wasn't being fair to the rest of the staff, which had to cover for Eve, pick up the slack for her when she was absent or late, and put up with her gossip and lies.

Teresa knew she was accountable for allowing Eve to disrupt her department, and she fired her. And then her other associates vilified her for it. Eve, they said, deserved more compassionate treatment because of her challenging personal life. "There were people who had voodoo dolls that looked like me," Teresa recalls. "And one of my best friends called me a 'cold-hearted b*tch.'"

But she stood her ground. Her personal support of Eve had come at a cost to the rest of the staff, to the department, and to Jen, whom Eve didn't respect. Teresa figured it wasn't fair to the associates who show up on time, tell the truth, and have a good attitude about work, even if the one who lost her job was their friend. In fact, Teresa admits now, she should have fired her sooner.

Instead, she offered to change Eve's hours to accommodate her new responsibilities as a single mom. She gave her monthly pep talks and told her she needed to improve her attendance, her attitude, and her performance. She handed her a written warning. She explained exactly what Eve needed to do to keep her job, even after Eve chose again and again not to do those things. Teresa worried about Eve and wondered why she chose not to make it work. Finally, she fired her.

And Teresa told her why. It was a brave conversation. It went something like this: "Everyone has a life outside of work. Everyone suffers through something at some point: deaths, divorce, illness, financial challenges, or family demands. Not everyone reacts to those things by slacking off at work and trying to demean her colleague who earned the managerial position."

Accountability, Teresa notes, comes from the top-down. Being an effective leader means being perfectly clear about what is expected of associates, and then holding those associates accountable for meeting those clear expectations when they are not being accountable for them. If an associate chooses not to meet them, the accountable leader has an obligation to transition him or her out of the firm.

Some on the staff have a lingering resentment toward Teresa; they think she kicked Eve while she was down. Still, months later, Teresa knows she did the right thing.

As a member of the company's executive team, Teresa is accountable for maintaining an associate-friendly environment. Enabling underperformers for a continuous period of time is not conducive to maintaining the firm's good reputation among associates and potential employees. It's not conducive to making it a comfortable, productive, and professional place to work.

As Teresa instructed Eve to pack up her desk and leave the building, Teresa could barely look her long-time associate in the eye. Yet as she watched her fired colleague drive out of the associate parking lot for the last time, she admits, she felt a huge relief from the months-long stress that came with her choice to keep Eve on board.

That's no surprise. When you maintain a mindset of accountability, you lower your stress.

Accountability is key to success—for a person, a team, a project, or an organization. Still, too few leaders hold themselves accountable for holding *others* accountable, even if they know they—and those they hold accountable—will be more successful if they do.

The reason? Maybe you don't hold somebody accountable because you're concerned about the person's happiness and you don't want to upset anyone. Or maybe you are letting less-than-accountable behavior slide because you don't want to be perceived as a "cold-hearted b*tch," as Teresa described. But are you really more concerned about the happiness of a friend, child, colleague, or associate than you are about his or her success? Are those whispers behind your back more important to you than your organization's success?

If you hold others accountable—and ask them to hold you accountable—you could find yourself ridiculed, gossiped about, even called names.

So what? It doesn't make accountability wrong. It doesn't make you wrong. It doesn't make the result of your actions wrong. You're cold-hearted because you asked someone to honor a commitment, meet a deadline, show up for work on time, or use sick leave only for an illness and not for a shopping trip? You're mean, stubborn, inflexible, or whatever other adjectives your associates come up with to describe your audacity at requiring them to bring in new clients or make a minimum number of sales?

Sounds like their problem, not yours.

Chances are good that those doing the name-calling are the same people who fall short of their sales goals every quarter—and then blame you for it. Or they blame the company, or their colleagues, or prospects who don't return calls, or their spouses, or the bad weather. They're the same ones who refuse to acknowledge that their "numbers"—from sales, to finished projects, to take-home pay—depend on how many people they call and visit each day, how many hours they put in, and how diligently they are about following up with clients and closing deals. They refuse to admit that their long lunches and hours surfing the Web are stealing time and effort from the outcome they have agreed to deliver.

They're the ones who say, long after making the agreement, that the expectation was unreasonable and that nobody could ever live up to your standards—even though many others easily do. They don't want you to hold them accountable any more than they hold themselves accountable. They find it easier to blame you and your rules for their failures. They find it easier to convince themselves that their shortcomings are someone else's fault.

So you write them up, put them on probation, hand them warnings, and even fire them. You do that because you *are* accountable.

Teresa could have done what was popular—let Eve continue her disruptive behavior until her personal life smoothed out. If she had taken this path, nobody would have called her cold-hearted. Instead, she empowered herself—with some prodding from her CEO—to fire Eve, even though she knew she risked some backlash from the woman's sympathetic colleagues. Teresa accepted the consequence of being branded as cold-hearted. She knows that accountable decisions rarely make everyone happy, and that business—and life—is not a popularity contest.

That's Where Winners Live.

She endured a few days as the butt of office gossip, but Teresa also knew it would blow over once the staff realized they no longer had to cover for Eve, pick up her slack, or try to slither away from her when she started her diatribes about Jen. And that's what happened. In the end, Teresa's accountable choice was perceived by nearly everyone as more than fair, both to Eve and to the rest of the staff. She was perceived as fair and concerned about the other associates and about the company.

That's a reputation she can live with.

Many corporate leaders are reluctant to act accountably when it means holding an underperformer, a trouble-maker, or an irresponsible associate accountable. In fact, it took a recession for many leaders finally to trim dead weight from their staffs. They needed an excuse—the recession—to do what a brave conversation could have handled for them long ago.

Now that the cuts have been made and staffs are leaner, good leaders are accountable for keeping their organizations running efficiently without unnecessarily padding the staff—even when the economy is strong.

Accountable leaders are brave enough to communicate the truth to employees, even when those conversations are uncomfortable. It's difficult to confront employees with their shortcomings, and it's even more difficult to say goodbye to those who have been long-time colleagues. Accountability, sometimes, is indeed a b*tch.

31

PAIN POINT: RESCUE, FIX, AND SAVE

Too many leaders are stuck in the weeds. Take James, a human resources director who just can't let his organization's associates work out their own problems. He wants to know about every squabble between co-workers and every tense moment between boss and subordinate.

He believes it's a bad idea for associates to talk to each other when they're having problems. It's important to him that they bring those issues to him instead of trying to work them out on their own. So they do. They run to him to resolve every little tiff. That's fine with their managers, who are happy to be off the hook for dealing with their own subordinates and to let James handle their staff problems for them.

Neither the associates nor their managers have bothered to—or have had any reason to—learn how to deal with upsets or to prevent them. They leave it to James to rescue, fix, and save them. That's fine with James, who fears he might not have enough to do if he didn't have that role. If nobody needed him to intervene, it's possible nobody would need him at all. That could leave him without a job.

Are you elbow-deep in the minutia of your business? Do you refuse to let your associates and managers clean up their own messes?

Step back for a minute and consider this: What would your life be like if you got out of the weeds? How much time would you have for other business and personal pursuits if you stopped looking over the shoulders of your sales force, checking call sheets, ticking off productivity, taking calls that someone with less seniority could easily handle, offering your two cents, and preventing the staff you so carefully hired and trained from taking care of the details while you focus on the big picture?

Where would you be? On the golf course three mornings a week? At the board meetings of the nonprofits and associations you volunteer to serve? On a cruise ship with your family? With students and young professionals who look to you for mentoring and advice? Or would you be unneeded and unemployed?

Sure, you complain about the interruptions and the frustration of having to micromanage associates and projects when you've delegated that role to others. What else can you do, after all, when you see empty offices at 9 A.M. and falling call sheet numbers? Or how about when you suspect that could happen, and you're the only one who can prevent it? You have to be involved on a nitty-gritty level, after all, to maintain a high level of performance among your staff, right?

Maybe not. If instead of doing the work you've hired others to do, what would happen if you set clear expectations for the results you want, and then you left it to the sales professionals and managers to own those goals and see them through? If instead of telling your staff how to do every job, what would happen if you described, in detail, your desired outcome of the effort, and then let the team figure out how to accomplish it? If instead of asking them what they think they need to do to produce a certain outcome—even though you already know what you're going to require them to do, no matter what they say— what would happen if you genuinely solicited their input and allowed them to try out their ideas?

Here's what would happen: The accountable associates you so carefully hired would figure it out. They would achieve the required result. They would succeed. And you would have all the time in the world to pursue bigger and different goals.

How does that sound? In fact, it sounds fairly scary to a lot of leaders, especially those who have made a career out of rescuing, fixing, and saving. Rescuing, fixing, and saving your associates from every little thing keeps a leader from being bored. It helps a leader feel needed, and that feels great.

If nobody needed you to do that, maybe you would be bored and feel unneeded. So you reap a great reward from rescuing, fixing, and saving. Perhaps you even set up your associates for it by neglecting to do strategic planning or neglecting to be clear about your expectations. Then, when the associates fall short of your unexpressed expectations, you can swoop in and save the day.

If that's working for you and your company, keep doing it. If it's not working, consider what you would do if you had more time, if your associates and managers didn't need saving so often—or ever—and if you didn't make everybody else's job your job.

Are you sweating? Is your heart palpitating? Do you need to sit down? Can't think of anything? Terrified that you might not be needed? Stop taking it out on your associates.

Few things frustrate high-performing associates more than a leader who tells them they're free to make decisions and figure out how to get things done—and then treats them like they need their hands held for the simplest tasks. The leader says, "I empower you." Then, as soon as the associate takes action, the leader says, "No, do it this way instead."

Miguel, a one-time firefighter, owns a fire/flood remediation company that contracts with insurance companies to salvage, demolish, and rebuild houses, condominiums, and office spaces after a disaster. He earns an average of $250,000 per job, and he meets his often-emotional clients under devastating circumstances.

He tells his associates they "own" their crews. He "empowers" them with permission to make concessions to clients and decisions when the day's work steers off course. But the second a client calls to clarify something with Miguel or ask for his input, the boss is in his car, headed for the job site. He's terrified that a client might be offended or dissatisfied, so he hurries over there to rescue, fix, and save the day—instead of trusting the crew to handle it.

During his drive over, he mulls over the wisdom of giving the crews so much authority. "If I had been in charge," he reasons with satisfaction, "we wouldn't be getting this type of call from clients."

Miguel hires well. His forty-employee firm includes top-notch sales professionals, decorated former firefighters, experienced builders, and former building code officials. He wouldn't keep them on the job if he couldn't trust him. He does trust them. Yet he runs to their rescue as if he doesn't.

That has nothing to do with trust. That's just a smoke screen he uses so he can continue to meddle. The fact is, if his crew could take care of everything without him, he wouldn't have anything to do.

Why wouldn't he like that? He says that's what he wants. He says he wants to semi-retire by age fifty to travel with his wife and spend more time with his adult children. But he acts like he's afraid to leave the business in the capable hands of his associates, some who have worked there for twenty-plus years.

Miguel is living the lie of "How Do I?" How do I leave the crew in charge when I get calls from clients who want to talk to me and only me? How do I possibly take an extended vacation when there's nobody here who can run the business for me? A better question might be: Why don't I let the crew handle it when I know they're just as capable as I am? Or: Why don't I get on a plane and go enjoy myself for a week or two?

Deep down, Miguel knows he can trust his crew. What he hasn't figured out is why he pretends that he doesn't. It could be that he's imagining a big, black hole of boredom. Or he fears his company will succeed without him, or that the crew really can resolve the client's issue without his help.

The problem here is not that Miguel doesn't trust his people. It's that his people don't trust Miguel to let go and let them do what they are capable of doing. The problem isn't trust as much as it is ego.

Ouch.

Why not make full disclosure to yourself and your associates and save both of you some worry and resentment? If you're a micromanager or a control freak and you want everyone to do what you say, let everyone know. Then the crew will call you before the client has a chance to do it. The crew will know you want to handle every little upset on the job site. And you'll get to do that. Then you'll stop slowing the boat down by throwing the anchor in every time your crew finds its rhythm.

Don't live the lie of "How Do I?" Don't pretend you don't trust your associates. The accountable action is full disclosure.

On the other hand, if you really want to go on vacation with your family more than you want to solve client problems, allow your crew to get some experience on their own with prickly clients. And then get on the plane.

How many times a day do you ask yourself or someone else, "How do I . . . ?" How do I tell my brother-in-law that I don't want to hire his son? How do I get these young associates to dress appropriately for work?

Are you asking so someone else will decide for you how to handle your own business? Are you making sure you have someone to blame in case the conversation or confrontation you're dreading doesn't go well? Don't ask. Act. Do what you already know how to do.

If Miguel's worst fears are realized, his company will flourish while he enjoys his semi-retirement and his family. So what's the problem?

32

PAIN POINT: DO IT MY WAY

Charles, a CEO, knows that if the sales professionals on his staff follow the same formula he did when he was in their position, they will earn all the money they want for themselves and for his company.

You can't argue with his results. He's successful. He's wealthy. He's a happy man. He owns a huge company. He credits his own personal accountability for his success. He is accountable to himself, his results, and the forty phone calls he made every single day as he earned his way to the top.

He lives Where Winners Live—in a world where success is built on personal accountability.

Now that he oversees hundreds of other sales professionals, he aims to create an environment for that kind of self-accountability to thrive. He wants to create a staff of "Mini-Me's." He wants his staff to be accountable for finding success the same way he did.

That tried-and-true formula is his secret weapon. It's the reason he's the boss. And that's true of most superstar sales professionals who become leaders. They earned that top spot by being top producers. They got there because of volume, not because of their ability to manage people or to lead an organization.

Managers and executives in sales are different from CEOs of hospitals or of most publicly traded companies, who might have risen through the ranks because of their expertise in a particular field or their impressive education, or because they worked for another successful company. In sales, the path to the top is a wide-open field. Personality and production are key to success.

Successful sales professionals often are driven by different motivators than professionals in other fields. Most thrive on competition, love spending their time with people, and covet the kind of lifestyle the perks and paycheck of a thriving sales career can buy them.

Every successful, executive-level sales professional knows exactly how he or she got to the top. And these leaders aim to motivate those coming up behind them to use the same tools and tactics so they can be successful, too. The success of those who are working their way up ensures that the executives will continue to be successful, too, as the managers, the leaders, and the organization all profit from every sale made by a sales professional affiliated with them. So they generously hand down their selling secrets.

Sometimes that works, and sometimes it doesn't. It turns out that the next-generation sales force has a different idea of accountability, of success, and of how to get there than many of those who sit in the C-suite today.

As a leader who knows that your way works, how comfortable are you with young go-getters who have their own ideas about what *else* might work? Is your way really the only way? Is the model that made you so very successful the only model that can drive sales, lead to success, make your associates rich, and fuel the company's growth?

Nobody can dispute that the tried-and-true model of making forty phone calls a day and meeting with ten potential new clients a week will poise even the greenest sales professional for blast-off from I'm Getting There to I Have Arrived. Nobody can deny that many forty-, fifty- and sixty-year-olds have successfully used that model to fatten their wallets, climb up through the ranks into leadership positions, and create comfortable lives for themselves and their families that far outshine anything their parents could have dreamed of.

It's also true that many twenty-somethings are happily gluing their seats to their chairs and their ears to their headsets, following that age-old road to riches, and quickly boosting themselves into the money very early in their sales careers.

So what happens when a promising young salesman wants to work with laser focus all morning and afternoon, and then clock out at 4 P.M. every day so he can devote as much attention to his personal life as to his career? What happens when a computer-savvy Gen-Y newcomer wants to work her 1,000-plus Facebook friends for leads and use e-mail or tweets instead of in-person meetings to close deals?

Before you answer those questions, consider another question: What if all of those tactics work? As a CEO, would you still insist that they employ the forty-phone-calls-a-day strategy if they were bringing in as much new business through social networks—either in person or online? If they are accountable for their numbers, does it matter that they added them up using a calculator you've never tried before? Do you hold them accountable for their results, *or for the way they achieve those results?*

If a newbie chooses to start her workday at 10 A.M. instead of 8 A.M. and still makes her numbers, are you going to lock her office door every morning so she has to ask you for the key and explain her schedule to you every day? Do you believe she is not accountable because her routine is different from the one that got you to where you are today? Do you view her colleague as not accountable because she meets her quotas day after day by mining her Facebook friends instead of by making phone calls? Is the top performer on her team less accountable because he relies on his highly efficient work style to succeed rather than on evening hours?

These are questions that every leader has to answer, and not just today. Each generation has its own ideas and its own way of doing things. Each generation has its own familiar tools and technology—and perhaps you did not have access to those same devices when you were building your success using methods that work as well today as they did ten, twenty, or thirty years ago.

Does that mean the new stuff can't work, too?

Many newcomers to the sales profession come with this mind-set: Accountability equals results, not process. And this mindset: Accountability equals results, not face time. If you believe that, it might be time for a change in your company's culture. It might be time to change the question you are asking, from, "Where are you?" to "What result are you getting?"

Change can be painful. But there is good news: In a one-size-doesn't-fit-all workplace, your way still fits like a glove. It's just not the only way that fits.

33

NON-NEGOTIABLES

Perhaps you are convinced that the "one-card" system of assigning points for each phone call and closed deal is the only system that will create accountable sales professionals and guarantee their success. After all, it made you a success, and it's clearly an effective system. If you believe it's the only effective system and you won't tolerate a member of your staff who deviates from it, make its use a condition of employment. And make that rule known to every associate, from Day 1 on the job.

Be clear with your staff that certain behaviors, schedules, and activities are non-negotiable, whether it's for the first six months on the job or forever. So, for example, if one of your non-negotiables is an 8 A.M. starting time, tell every sales associate, "I'll pay you X amount, and one of my non-negotiables is that you have to be in your office, at your desk, at 8 A.M. If you are late, I will lock your office door and you'll have to explain why you're late before I'll give you the key."

That's accountable. You set out clear expectations. You're not letting people assume it's OK to set their own hours, and then later complaining that Associate A never shows up until 10 A.M. The sales pro who doesn't want to start work at 8 A.M. knows it's non-negotiable and is accountable for choosing to stay with your firm or find one that offers flextime.

Same goes if your non-negotiable is forty phone calls a day, evening hours, and five sales per week. If you make your expectations clear, the people who work for you have the information they need to make accountable choices. They have the information they need to give informed consent. And they have an opportunity to meet your expectations. Only people who know the notes to your song, after all, will be able to sing along.

This kind of transparency will cost you some recruits, for sure. Not everyone embraces this kind of culture. But those who stick around—those who are accountable, at least—will value your experience and your strategy and will happily follow it in their quest to achieve the same success you have achieved.

Clear expectations alleviate a lot of stress and head off even more confusion, hard feelings, and disappointment.

The source of all disappointment and conflict, after all, is a missed expectation.

GO AHEAD: DO IT YOUR WAY

Another viable route is to let those you're nurturing find their own way and make their own mistakes. And nobody knows that better than Dave.

When Dave was a twenty-two-year-old newcomer to the insurance industry in 1983, he and a couple of other salesmen pitched in to buy a "robot" machine that made phone calls for them. The granddaddy of today's "robo-calls," the machine dialed a number, waited for someone to answer, and then paused for five seconds. Then a recording explained who Dave was, said he was calling about insurance, and asked whoever answered the phone to press 1 if he or she was not happy with the family's current insurance agent.

"We bought a machine to replace what I was supposed to do," laments Dave, who says he was convinced it would work by other agents who said it would garner more sales. It didn't.

Whether it's 1983 or 2013, if you answer your phone and hear a five-second delay, you hang up. If you're asked by a machine to give personal information because the sales professional can't be bothered to talk to you himself, you hang up the phone.

Today, when newcomers to the insurance industry tell Dave they're going to try something new or different to hit their numbers, he tells them to go ahead. "Maybe they have to learn it the hard way. But if they say, 'I'll do it my way,' and it doesn't work, then I want them to do it my way." When their sales figures come in, he can see just how well their way is working out.

It's the same thing with a fifteen-year-old who's doing homework. The dad wants her to do it the way he knows will get it done best. But she's fifteen, and she wants to do it her way.

Go ahead. Do it your way.

When the report card comes, we'll see if your way is working. If it's not working, then try doing it the way someone more experienced would do it.

When your sales figures come in, we'll see how well your way is working.

The most promising sales professionals, advisors, business owners, and fifteen-year-olds are eager for direction and advice. Still, most of them want the freedom to try out their own ideas.

Leaders at most insurance or financial firms expect new advisors to earn a specific amount of revenue by the end of their third full year with the organization. As a leader, what do you do if an advisor doesn't hit that number? Accountable leaders ask the advisor this question: What can we, as an organization, do to get you to where you need to be?

At Baystate, about 40 percent of advisors make their Year Three number. Of the remaining 60 percent, some have fabulous careers with the company, but they move at a slower pace. Some go away.

A lot of discussion occurs between each advisor and his or her manager along the way:

- What is an ideal week for you?
- How many people will you see?
- How many phone calls will you make?
- How will you spend your time?

Sales leaders know that 80 percent of a sales associate's time should be spent in activity, making appointments or going to appointments, for the first three years. Without substantial activity, any advisor is in trouble. If, for example, you want to sell disability insurance policies to doctors, how much time are you spending at the local hospital? How much time do you spend doing what will help you meet your goal? An experienced sales professional might say you should spend three days a week onsite at the hospital visiting with doctors.

There's no big secret about how to succeed in sales. It's about knowing what you want and then taking the action and the risks you need to reach that goal. The accountable sales professional will ask, "I know what I want. What am I doing to get it?" Accountable sales professionals know they are the only ones who can get for themselves what they want. They know they alone are accountable for achieving their personal and professional goals, for reaching their definitions of success.

Still, you, as the leader, can help. And if your admonitions about the "right way" fall on deaf ears, how about saying, "Go ahead, try it your way"? Let the pro with a good idea convince you that it will work. Let the eager newcomer show you it will result in $200,000-plus in earnings within three years.

Sales is an extremely high-risk business. At times, in fact, it might seem like high-risk surgery. If the surgeon, the nurses, and the anesthesiologist do everything they are supposed to do, the operation likely will succeed. But if any one of them drops the ball, the surgery will fail—and the team will fail.

Likewise, if the leadership and the company do everything they're supposed to do and the sales associate does everything he or she is supposed to do, both will be successful. If one or the other fails to do his or her part, all will fail, not just one or the other.

In this business, a leader can lay out a prescription for success, can offer training, and can prescribe work hours. The associate who heeds that plan is likely to be successful.

Some people, of course, want to use the "rich uncle system": My uncle says, "Here are my friends; just call them." But that's probably not a great system, given that most uncles don't have unlimited friends.

But is there one "right" system?

One system requires the sales professional or financial advisor to sit at her desk from 8 A.M. to 4 P.M. every day, talking with prospects on the phone, in person, or online in a place where the boss can see her at all times and know she's hard at work. For some, that's a great system. In another system, the boss says, "I don't have to see you. I don't have to talk to you. But I know the number we're after. If you're hitting that weekly number, I know you're doing the right thing." That's a viable way to reach your financial goals, too.

The reliable, leader-favored one-card system created many years ago is a third way to go. The advisor is required to earn twenty-five "points" a week from this tally:

- He earns half a point for each qualified prospect he identifies, often because someone has referred the person to him. He learns the person's name, address, date of birth, occupation, and other basic information.
- He gets one point for taking a fact-finder on somebody.
- He gets one point for a closing interview.
- He earns one point for having a meal with a client or potential client.

At the end of the week, if the associate has earned twenty-five points, and he does this consistently from week to week, it is proven in the sales industry that he will be successful. Those who accumulate fewer than fourteen points a week are likely to fail in the business.

In a fourth system, the leader says, "Go ahead and do it your way." It's not an open-ended system, but it's an open-minded system. It is not guaranteed to work, but it is not guaranteed to fail. It doesn't rely on a tried-and-true formula or a specific number of phone calls per week. And many, many leaders can't stomach it. It goes like this: The new sales professional has an idea for how to reach $200,000-plus in three years (or whatever your organization sets as its internal benchmark) that differs from yours. You say, "Go ahead and try it your way," and the two of you agree on short-term goals and weekly numbers. You'll both know in short order if the advisor's new idea is working—both for the advisor and for the company.

Here's an example: A brand-new, never-sold-anything-before financial manager wanted to show up for work at 11:30 A.M. four out of five mornings each week so she could spend her mornings playing golf. Her CEO balked, but agreed to allow it as long as she hit her numbers. About a year later, she had earned $106,000. Turns out, she's been meeting all kinds of financially comfortable hackers on the golf course who bought her product and referred her to their friends and colleagues. She did it her way, and it's been working for her.

Another newcomer, fortyish, pooh-poohed the traditional systems and said he was going to try hitting his numbers using a self-devised tracking system. It didn't work. The truth is, he didn't want to track his activity, and he didn't want anyone else tracking it, either. He just wanted to be left alone. It was clear within a few weeks that his "system" wasn't going to fly, and his boss cut it off.

What's the difference between the "hacker" and the "tracker," two people who started working for the same company on the same day, participated in the same training programs, and have the same access to the same company resources? The golfer is holding herself accountable for hitting her points every week. The tracker? No accountability.

In finance and insurance industry sales, as in so many businesses, where you are is simply the result of what you did to get there. Good leaders will intervene when results are poor. Many leaders will ask their struggling subordinates to account for their activity. They will ask the following questions:

- What activity did you engage in to achieve the results you're showing?

- Did you call 200 people this week? Check.
- Did you make a dozen appointments? Check.
- But you're still not hitting your numbers? *Call more people. Make more appointments.*

Highly accountable leaders take a different approach. They know that they are as much responsible for the success of the sales professionals whom they supervise as the professionals are for their own success. They see a poor result and they ask, "What resources can I provide to you so you get the result you want?" And then, they clarify their expectations: "Here is the result you have to produce to succeed with this company. Here is what I expect. Here are my non-negotiables."

Activity is important to achieve results. The "tracker" didn't fail because he didn't adopt a specific system, even a tried-and-true one. He failed because he didn't have a system at all; he didn't want to be held accountable, and he didn't hold himself accountable for his results.

Likewise, the golfer didn't fail, even though she strayed from the tried-and-true system. The difference: She is accountable for her results, no matter how they materialize. And her CEO got what he wanted—results. If her CEO wanted specific activity instead of specific results, she might not have stayed with that company.

That CEO doesn't spend much of his time checking to make sure his advisors are sitting at their desks by 8 A.M. He doesn't waste his energy being frustrated that they don't arrive in the office on time or blaming them for underperformance because of it, because 8 A.M. isn't important to him; $200,000 by the end of the third year, however, is important. His focus is the result.

Likewise, this CEO doesn't have a pat answer for every advisor who comes to him with a problem. He doesn't say, "Just follow this system and everything will work out." Instead, he says, "Let's figure this out. Talk to me about what you think needs to happen. What can you do to make that happen? *What can I do to help you?"*

Not for you? That's OK, too—as long as your sales staff knows this. If you say, "I want you to think for yourself, devise a strategy, and own your results," your advisors will do that. If what you *mean*, however, is, "That's all true as long as the strategy you devise is the one I want you to use, and as long as I see lots of evidence that you're doing it my way." That, of course, would reveal a bold lie on your part. And once that lie is exposed, people will start leaving your organization.

Same goes for any promise you make to your associates or to your recruits. Attracting sales recruits to your organization by promising flexibility and the opportunity for them to be their own bosses is just "lipstick on a pig" if the truth is that you're going to flip the first time they don't make it to their desks by 8 A.M. If you tell them, "Look at my top producers who get to vacation with their families in Aruba and Hawaii on the company's dime," but hide the fact that even those superstars made only $60,000 during their first year on the job and had to work every weekend for it, you're not giving your recruits the chance to make the best decision about whether to accept the job.

Sure, coming clean up-front with recruits will scare some of them away. So decide: When do you want your pain? Before you invest in training your newcomers, or after they've been on the job for a few months and have figured out that the rewards take time but the hard work and personal sacrifices are immediate?

CHAPTER

35

PAIN POINT: CLARITY

The leader of a multi-million-dollar division of a publicly traded organization says it has been years since the division has achieved its strategically planned targets. He has a mindset of personal accountability, so he looked inward for a solution to his problem rather than trying to blame it on his staff.

His revelation: He wasn't making his expectations clear to those who work for him. He wasn't setting benchmarks, revealing his non-negotiables, and getting buy-in from those he expected to do the work.

Unclear expectations are the bane of a leader's existence, both in the giving and in the getting. A leader who communicates unclear expectations is a conflict avoider. And a conflict avoider, of course, is not a leader.

Before you can be clear with your staff about your expectations, review those expectations and ask the following questions:

- Is what you are expecting doable?
- Are the resources available?
- Are the roles clear?
- Is authority established in each role?
- Is this group supposed to work as a team or in a "chain of command"?

- Has the group had an opportunity to ask questions and even push back until each team member can say, "I own this fully"?

Get a "yes" to each of these questions, and then you can say, as a leader, "Let me be clear. We are capable of this. Meet the expectation or expect not to be here. I will not rescue, fix, and save underperformers as I have in the past, and I will ensure, from now on, that I am available so you can bring me any issues that your team is unable to resolve. Let's work together. If one of us fails, we all fail."

If you, as the leader, are not clear with yourself about your own expectations, get clear before you make any assignment.

Few things are more frustrating to a high-performing sales professional than wishy-washy instructions. Constantly changing your mind about when something is due or what must be included in the final product tells your associates that the deadline is flexible or that they can decide when to finish the work. It frustrates team members who depend on their colleagues to get Step A finished in time for Step B to begin.

Others might be comfortable with a suggestive style and can "go with the flow," not knowing if or when they will be caught halfway through a project that is needed immediately. Still, in a business with a bottom line or with shareholders to answer to, the leader must be clear about his or her leadership style. There's nothing wrong with hiring associates who work well with suggestions and only occasional clear directions. That might work for your company, as long as the associates who come on board understand that's how you run things. Let people know what they are in for, so they can opt out if your style and your company's culture won't work for them.

Ask yourself the following questions:

- Has it been years since your division or organization has hit its metrics?

- Do you spend more time as a leader firefighting than offering strategies where you are needed?
- Have you learned the concept of accountability but still don't hold people accountable?
- Do you remain poor at setting clear expectations because you fear people will call you an inflexible tyrant who is hard to work for?

Accountability can be a puzzle. Be accountable and figure yourself out.

PAIN POINT: I CAN'T KNOW EVERYTHING

36

In case after case in the news, leaders of organizations are asked what they knew about unsavory and unethical acts in their companies and when they knew it. Their standard, carefully worded response is, "I don't recall."

Right. They don't have any recollection of anything involved in the worst calamity to hit the company in its history?

You probably don't believe them any more than we do. But who cares? In fact, in these instances of outrage, why do we care about, "When did you know?" We're asking the wrong question. The right question is, "Are you accountable?"

Even if a leader, whether it be Penn State's Joe Paterno, Enron's Kenneth Lay, or News Corporation's Rupert Murdoch, said, "Yes, I knew, and I made a note right here in my calendar about the day I was told," what good would that do anybody? How would that resolve a problem or change the situation going forward?

Everyone in the audience, of course, would have to pick themselves up off the floor to finish uploading their video clips to YouTube, where the stunning admission would go viral within minutes.

But what happens next would be much the same as what happens when those same leaders say, "No, I had no idea that this was going on right under my nose." The story would take on a life of its own, the lawyers would all get paid, and the leaders would still lose their jobs or have to answer for themselves to the authorities.

So why does it matter so much if the leader knew or not? Why is *that* the story? Why not focus that energy instead on learning what happened, how, and why, and on figuring out how to prevent it from ever happening again? Let's change the question from "Did you know?" to "Are you accountable?" The legal consequences likely will be the same whether the answer is yes or no. But a "Yes, I am accountable—whether I knew about it or not" leads to this: "Here is what I will do every day, from now on, to restore the company and the trust that my associates and the public have in me as a leader. This is why I deserve to keep my job while I go through any necessary legal process."

"No, I am not accountable for what I did not know about" means this: Fire up the legal fund. Prepare for a loss of business. Brace the associates for layoffs. Spend your time and energy dealing with regulators, opponents, and the media, who won't leave you alone until they find out whether you are lying.

The less personally accountable our leaders, our corporations, and we are, the more laws and regulations we need to *hold* us accountable. The more personally accountable we all are, the more we will all police our own behaviors and hold ourselves accountable, simply because we *are* accountable.

Professionals who work in a regulated industry, such as financial services, banking, or insurance, must comply with state, federal, and industry regulations designed to keep them honest, their transactions transparent, and their practices legal. The highly accountable professional, though, defines compliance as more than oversight and requirements. Winners define compliance as doing the right thing—even when nobody is looking; even when there's no chance you could get caught if you did the wrong thing.

Compliance means treating your clients right and putting their interests first. Compliance means honoring your fiduciary responsibility to your clients and your employer. Sounds a lot like personal accountability.

In fact, the more personally accountable you are, the fewer rules and regulations you need from the government, from your industry, or from your company to make sure you do the right thing. The more you treat others as you would like to be treated, the less likely you are to cross any legal or ethical line that would trigger an investigation into your behavior.

As a high school student, Dave worked as a driver for a funeral home owned by the grandfather of a girlfriend. So when his own father died suddenly in 1996, he had an idea of what to expect when he accompanied his mother and sister to make the arrangements. After hearing the sales pitch by the funeral director, Dave asked his mother to leave the room. He said to the director, who had tried his best to take advantage of the family's grief and oversell the funeral, "Are you kidding me? Just do the right thing. Here's what my mother can afford. Why are you pushing her to overspend on things she doesn't need?"

That funeral director's definition of compliance probably included the words "only if I get caught." This "got-caught accountability" is not 100 percent personal accountability. It's not the mindset Where Winners Live. Winners don't need laws to remind them that they are accountable to their clients, their businesses, and themselves. Winners don't need to fear they will get caught doing something they're not supposed to be doing—because they either are not doing it or they stand up, admit it, and accept the consequences of any underhanded actions they chose to take.

If everyone had the mindset of 100 percent personal accountability, rules like the financial services industry's federally audited "suitability" standard would be unnecessary. The requirement mandates that any product a financial advisor sells to a client has to be suitable for the client. Suppose, for example, that a client tells her financial planner that she wants to invest a large sum of money but she will need to have access to those funds three years from now. It would be inappropriate for that advisor to convince her to invest in a fund with a huge withdrawal penalty, even if it would mean he could collect a heftier commission on that sale than on one that would allow the client to withdraw her money without penalty.

In that case, the advisor has helped himself but hurt his client. That's not suitable for the client. And it's not legal. If the advisor defined compliance as winners do—treating clients right and putting their interests first—he would be accountable for offering only suitable investment opportunities to his clients.

If every advisor defined compliance as honoring his fiduciary responsibility to the clients and the employer, those who enforce the suitability standard would have nothing to do. A standard or a law can't "make" you accountable. You are or you aren't. A standard or a law can't "make" you honest. Be accountable. Be honest. Don't oversell. Don't cut corners. If you are not accountable to yourself and your clients, it will come back to bite you.

Sandra, the director of a financial planning department for a hybrid firm that sells insurance and provides financial planning services, was unhappy with her salary, but her boss denied her a raise. So she chose to quit her job, and she started working for a bank that also offered financial planning services. She secretly took her old company's client list with her.

After contacting sixty-six clients on that list by sending them letters on the bank's stationary, she was cited by government regulators for violating securities laws, privacy laws, and her non-compete agreement with the first company. Now, her former employer and the bank—now also a former employer—are in settlement talks, with big money at stake. And Sandra owes more than $10,000 in legal bills.

Here's another example to consider: Two relatively new employees of an accounting/financial planning practice got involved in a Ponzi scheme. They knew they were skirting the system and banking greater-than-expected profits for themselves and their clients, but they claimed they trusted the owner of the company that was investing their clients' money. Plus, they thought they were a little bit smarter than the average investment advisor and had a better way to make money. They thought that instead of putting one foot in front of the other to reach their goals, they would jump ten steps ahead of everyone else and take a shortcut.

The owner of the other company turned out to be a crook; he got caught and went to jail. The two accountants are still accountants, but they are no longer financial advisors; they were fired by the financial services firm they were affiliated with and government regulators will not allow them to work elsewhere as advisors.

The CEO of that financial services firm did not know these two affiliated accountants were involved in a Ponzi scheme. That firm carefully reviews all e-mails sent by its affiliates, and compliance officers there did not know that the accountants had set up private, outside e-mail accounts to use when they conducted the shady side of their business.

The firm complied with the law and followed its own procedures. A member of the firm's compliance team visited the affiliates' office twice a year, just as it does with all affiliates. And, still, the accountants engaged in fraud. The CEO of the financial services team did not go on TV to deny his accountability or to make sure everyone knew he didn't know what the accountants were cooking up behind his back. Instead, he fired them. He analyzed what happened. He brainstormed with the compliance experts at his firm. And he tightened the firm's practices beyond what government regulations require, checking outside e-mail accounts, spot-checking the files of affiliates, and doubling its efforts to keep abreast of what's going on in every affiliated office.

"Unfortunately," notes the CEO, "we're in a business where if somebody wants to skirt the system, they will do it." But it's far less likely they'll do it on his watch in the future. His new practice: trust and verify.

That's Where Winners Live.

Leader, own what's yours. What happens on your watch is yours. Stand up and say so. Admit it. Learn from it. Do better next time because of it. Show *that* to the media and to the public. Watch *that* go viral on the Internet.

Demonstrate accountability. Own your results—and the results of those who work for you—whether they are good or bad. Eliminate your need for the spin doctors who feed the monster of memos and media and manipulative public statements that really say nothing but, "I need a lawyer."

Let's arm ourselves with the best answers to the questions that monster is asking:

- This is what I did.
- This is what I learned.
- This is what I will do differently in the future.
- This is how I am accountable for what happened and how I will be accountable in the future.

A story without any fault, blame, or guilt is tough to tell. Yet it's much more interesting and useful than one full of denials and finger-pointing. It's certainly more unique. Even in controversy, lead by example. Lead by accountability.

Isn't that the kind of leader you want the people in your company to follow?

OUTCOME EQUALS INTENTION

> "Finding the answer isn't as important as being
> willing to consider the question."
>
> —*Linda Galindo, accountability thought leader,*
> *speaker, coach, consultant, author*

True leaders—and true winners—are accountable for their decisions, their choices, their behavior, their actions, and, most important, their outcomes. That includes all of their outcomes: good or bad, expected or stunning, welcome or disappointing.

Winners are accountable for their outcomes even when those results are the opposite of what they said they intended. That's because true winners know that outcomes reveal true intentions. So it follows that winners are accountable for their intentions—even their subconscious intentions. True winners know they are accountable for every thought in their heads—and how those thoughts influence their results, even if they didn't expect them.

Winners who operate at the highest level of personal accountability know that their accountability does not stop with what they say they want—or with what they can control. Accountability doesn't stop, period. At the end of the day, when you look at your results, you know that is what you are accountable for. You aren't accountable for your hopes and dreams or for your stated intentions; you are accountable for your results.

You can say circumstances beyond your control—like the actions of someone else—thwarted your intentions and spoiled your outcomes. You can believe that to be true with every waking thought. Still, what happened did happen. The outcome is the outcome. And like it or not, it's yours—all yours. You knew it would be yours, and yet you got a result you swore you did not want.

Wrap your head around that for a minute. Then answer this: *Would you consider that you actually intended a bad outcome?* Or at least an outcome that's different from what you were convinced you wanted? Most people won't consider that. Most people don't live Where Winners Live, willing to be 100 percent personally accountable for every one of their outcomes, no matter how bizarrely off-course it might seem.

Are you willing to admit that on some level, an odd, bad, or disappointing outcome is what you actually intended? That what you produced is what you intended, even if it's not what you said you wanted—or even if it is what you specifically said you did not want? Don't answer until you read Linda's story about why she intended to be an hour late for a speech to an audience of 200 people.

Hoping to impress a big new client, Linda had traveled from her Utah home to Philadelphia to address the company's highest level managers about how personal accountability can help them become more productive. Her husband traveled with her, and he chose to stay at their hotel while she gave her speech. Still, he insisted on giving her directions for a shortcut to the meeting that he swore would shorten her trip.

Linda had already mapped out the trip, choosing a route that she felt comfortable driving. Using her plan, she would drive at a leisurely pace, keep herself calm so she would arrive composed and ready to face the audience, have plenty of time to recover if she happened to take a wrong turn, and still reach her destination almost two hours early.

As she was walking out the door, her husband handed her a road map and showed her an alternative route. She questioned the wisdom of following his directions and argued that she wanted to go the way she had already chosen. He argued his position, which dredged up for Linda every negative incident involving a man and a map that she had ever endured: her parents fighting in the car about being lost, even though they had a map; her husband insisting on prior occasions that there was no need to stop to ask for directions, even though he had driven miles off course.

Still, she took his map and she drove his way. She was an hour late for her speech.

An unhappy audience waited for her. She took the stage and started her presentation, which went something like this: "What you produce, and not what you say, is what you intend." A woman in the audience stood up and shouted, "So you intended to be an hour late?" Linda froze, even though she never freezes in front of audiences.

"Of course not," she said after an awkward silence. "I would never do that." And she believed it—for a second. But as soon as she choked out the words, she realized she was lying. If she had to be honest, she would have to admit that it was more important to prove her husband wrong about his directions than to be on time. She could have chosen to drive the roads she felt comfortable with instead of taking her husband's advice, which she suspected might get her lost.

When that penny dropped, the truth about just how stubborn she could be in order to make him "wrong" played out in her head. On some level, she realized, getting lost and being late were her choices. It was more important for her to prove this man and his map wrong than it was for her to be on time for a speech to 200 high-ranking executives who work for her brand-new client. She would rather blow the contract, lose the client, and humiliate herself in front of a crowd of strangers than allow her husband to win an argument about a map. Her result revealed her intention. She didn't know that until the woman in the audience asked her if she intended to be late.

Likewise, you might not realize that you intended to get fired from your last job, lose the big client you'd been chasing for months, or miss out on a company-paid trip to the tropics by just a sale or two. Stop shaking your head. Just hear us out.

Linda was late because she chose to follow her husband's directions instead of her own. Yet her husband isn't accountable for her arriving an hour late. Linda is accountable. Whether her husband was wrong about the directions or not, Linda is the one who was late. She's the one who is accountable. She's the one frozen on the stage in front of 200 angry executives.

Is that what she wanted? Maybe not quite. But she wanted her husband to be wrong more than she wanted to be on time. Her results proved that. Outcome equals intention. So, in the end, she got what she intended. If she had any intention to be on time and impress her audience, it wasn't as important as proving her husband wrong.

Here's another example: A division vice president for a huge financial services firm has not signed off on a strategic plan for his section in four years. A perfectionist, he refuses to issue the plan until he is absolutely certain that each facet of it is achievable. That, of course, might be impossible to ascertain until the plan is in place and plays out over time. But the VP is risk-averse when it comes to his career, and he doesn't want to be blamed for a poor decision. So he won't enforce a plan.

Without a strategic blueprint, the division's high-level managers lack focus, so they are each doing their own thing. And without a plan, there's no system for dealing with underperforming investments or disgruntled clients. Predictably, the division is in disarray and the company is suffering as a result.

Looking from the outside in, it seems the VP intends for the division—and by extension, the company—to fail. Yet he swears he wants success for both. He says he intends for his division to shine and the company to profit, even as it falters as the result of poor planning.

The outcome is failure. So how can his intentions yield success?

When pressed, the VP has to admit that his stated intention—success—is overshadowed by his need for certainty. His true intention is to avoid personal and professional risk, even if it means the company fails. He made the choice.

Outcome equals intention.

And here's one last example: Suppose Linda had been an hour late for her speech because her plane to Philadelphia, which was supposed to arrive six hours before her appointment, made an emergency landing because of a mechanical failure. She did everything she possibly could to get on another flight so she would make it to her meeting on time, yet despite her best efforts, she arrived late.

Did she intend to be an hour late? In this scenario, she hasn't argued with her husband. She doesn't have a clear, competing intention that turns out to be more important than honoring her commitment to give a speech at a certain time.

Still, don't say "no" so fast.

Think about it first. Really consider whether there is any possible reason—even a subconscious one—that would make Linda get on a plane that had to make an emergency landing.

Is the question ridiculous? Are you willing to consider it anyway? True winners are. Truly accountable people are always game to look at an unexpected result and wonder what they might have done differently to prevent it. They're always willing to figure out what lesson they can learn from a failure so that it won't happen again. They're always willing to ask the question: Did I intend this—on any level? Even subconsciously?

If you're lucky, the answer will be yes, at least sometimes. It's only when you dig that deep into yourself, into your most private thoughts and even into your subconscious, that you will elevate yourself from a person who is very accountable—willing to own, say, 85 percent of your results, good or bad—to one who owns 100 percent of your outcomes without fault, blame, or guilt, because you know they all result from your choices and actions. Winners live at 100 percent. Winners *are at least willing to consider* that what they said is not what they intended; that, instead, what they produced is what they intended. They're willing to turn up the volume on that voice in their heads that's saying, "You knew something was off. You could have spoken up. You could have turned right instead of left. You didn't trust your own instincts. You had the opportunity to change this outcome. You chose not to do so."

Winners are willing to look at every angle of a situation. It's that examination of what's not obvious that creates the breakthroughs that allow winners to benefit so much more from their missteps than those who refuse to shine this uncomfortable spotlight on their true intentions.

Some people will become defensive when confronted with the notion that outcome equals intention. They'll say the issue is ridiculous and will refuse to consider it. They will blame forces beyond their control—without even examining how they, themselves, might have brought those forces into play through their subtle manipulation of the situation, through an off-handed remark, a snap decision, or their out-of-character reaction to someone or something, for example. They won't learn and grow from the surprises, disappointments, and troubles they experience.

In the case of Linda and the airplane, she genuinely considered a possible intention for being late. Maybe, deep down, she really didn't want to give the speech. Or maybe the plane just had a faulty valve, and it didn't have anything do with Linda or anyone else on board. Nobody but Linda will ever truly know what Linda's intentions were. And she is convinced there is nothing she could have done differently to change the outcome. She's OK with that.

If, after deep introspection following a poor outcome, your most honest, most private answer is, "No, that bad outcome absolutely was not my intention," then simply move on.

Finding the answer isn't as important as being willing to consider the question. So go through the introspection, every time. Live Where Winners Live. Consider your results the same as your intentions. Put yourself into the rigor of the question. Keep your answer private if you want. Admit it only to yourself. But tell yourself the straight truth about your intentions. You'll live at a much higher level if you do. You'll play at 100 percent personal accountability.

That is tough, and most people never get there. Those who do achieve 100 percent sometimes slip. In fact, most people play at a very low level of accountability, blaming even their most obvious foibles on bad luck and other people instead of owning the consequences of their own choices.

Perhaps this book has helped you elevate your own level of personal accountability so that you own at least 85 percent of every outcome you touch, and you assign no more than 15 percent of the responsibility for your success or failure to forces beyond your control. If you live at 85 percent accountability, you are on the road to Where Winners Live. It's a good path to travel.

Even if you never achieve 100 percent personal accountability—and few do, even though it is equally available to everybody—your quality of life at 85 percent is (or will be) so much better than it is or was at 25 percent or 50 percent. Even if you don't find a reason when you challenge yourself to admit that a poor outcome reflects your true intention, your willingness to ask yourself such a high-quality question will improve your future outcomes. It will make you a more careful thinker and will help you think before you act. It will help you act with intention so you get the results that you truly do intend.

This kind of thinking will lead you to be responsible for the success or failure of everything you do—for your choices, behaviors, and actions—*before* you know how it will all turn out; you'll own all of it, even if you're working for or with somebody else. The accountability mindset will propel you to empower yourself to succeed by taking the actions and risks that will ensure you achieve the results you desire. It will move you to demonstrate your willingness to answer for the outcomes that result from your choices, behaviors, and actions, without fault, blame, or guilt, no matter whether that outcome is good or bad. Every time.

That's Where Winners Live.

Where do you live?

Epilogue

If you live Where Winners Live, your constant, consistent, and unwavering personal accountability is what sets you apart from the sales professionals, wealth managers, bankers, and financial advisors who drag excuses and what-ifs around with them just in case they need something to blame if things go wrong.

But we're not here to pat you on the back for being accountable. We're here to remind you to wake up tomorrow and be accountable.

Winners don't celebrate their accountability. They don't even think about it. It's just who, what, and how they are.

Personal accountability is not something extra. It doesn't come and go. It's a state of being that reaps unlimited personal rewards, ranging from better relationships, to stress-free work days, to greater commissions, to happier clients. And it has never been more important for finance professionals than it is right now, when recession-weary investors—both wealthy and work-a-day—are grappling with the hit to their retirement savings accounts and fearing not only the shaky economy but the stock market, the banks, and even the advisors they want and need to trust with their money.

You know that markets ebb and flow. You know that the unending publicity about the crimes of a few unscrupulous financial professionals truly is about just a few and not most. You know that not every banking institution that accepted help from the federal government during the lowest of times mis-spent the money.

Your clients—and your prospects—don't know all of that. To them, this unfortunate perfect storm of a bad economy, a few bad apples, and a bad rap for the bank bailout is one bad event, and the culprits responsible are *all* who work in finance. So they're holding you accountable, no matter how far removed you, your practice, and the firms you're affiliated with might be from any hint of scandal or wrongdoing.

It doesn't matter if they're right. It matters what they think.

And for financial professionals who live Where Winners Live, dealing with the newly skeptical investor requires nothing more than what they already are: highly accountable for their own choices, behaviors, and actions. So don't spend a minute defending, apologizing, or even explaining what the scoun-drels in the news have done. You are not accountable for them. Instead, exude your own accountability. Exhibit trustworthiness. Emanate reliability. Behave likewise.

Your best tool is communication.

What follows are ten ways winning financial advisors and their clients are succeeding in an environment of skepticism and fear.

1. *Focus on your practice and your clients.* If a headline-making Ponzi scheme or bank failure is unlikely to affect your practice or your clients' portfolios, let your customers know—and then let it go. Like the performance of the stock market, scandals at other firms are beyond your control. Instead of spending your energy worrying or speculating about the troubles of oth-ers, devote yourself to taking action to protect your clients and manage their anxiety by keeping them informed about what is relevant to their money and what isn't.

2. *Keep in close touch with clients.* Make it a practice to meet—in person, if possible—with your wealthiest clients once every ninety days and with others twice a year. One successful advisor tells us he didn't lose a single A-list client

during the market meltdown of 2008 because every one of them was within forty-five days of a review—so they saw it coming. A missed expectation, after all, is the source of all upset. As upset as the clients might have been with their balance sheets, nobody blamed the advisor.

3. *Push for in-person meetings*. Phone calls and e-mails are great for between-meeting reminders, news blasts, and questions, but they are no substitute for the traditional, face-to-face portfolio review. Only a personal get-together allows both advisor and client to get to know the other, to respond to body language and facial expressions, and to establish a comfort level that invites trust on both sides. A face-to-face conversation, if it's in the advisor's office, also shows the client that the professional is just that—dressed for success, working in a nice office at a stable practice, and surrounded by enough support staff to handle financial planning needs well into the future.

4. *Use technology creatively*. In between face-to-face meetings, or when a personal meeting just isn't possible, use Skype or a video conferencing service so you and your client can at least see each other while you're talking. One clever advisor we know carries his laptop around his offices during these video meetings so each member of his team—from the person who answers his phone when he's away to the partner who can answer questions and take orders in his absence—can spend a couple of minutes chatting with the client during the call, and so the client can attach faces to what otherwise would be just voices and names.

5. *Involve your staff with every client*. That video-savvy advisor is onto something: Making clients and even prospects comfortable with every member of the team can go a long way toward relieving anxiety if the advisor is unavailable when the customer calls. Each staff member should know all clients' names, their level of business with the practice, and some personal information—such as whether they have

children and where they work—to use to break the ice and
remind clients that everyone in the office knows them
and is working for them.

6. *Help your clients get to know you.* One winning advisor in
Boston says he freely reveals information about his family,
his background, his values, and even his religion to clients, who, in turn, open up with him about their opinions,
dreams, and goals. It's not uncommon for him to receive
e-mails from clients who want to share their vacation
photos and see his. The give-and-take helps clients recognize that their financial advisor shares their values, which
builds trust and even friendships between them. In addition
to encouraging good relationships, this kind of bonding
makes clients comfortable referring friends and family members to your practice.

7. *Expect prospects to know a lot about you before you ever meet.*
The more skeptical someone is, the deeper he or she will
check you out before agreeing to the first meeting. Don't
be disarmed when someone starts chatting about your college or your spouse—with details about the year you gradu-
ated or got married. It's possible the prospect will have
checked with federal, state, and industry regulators to learn
about prior scuffles with clients or regulatory agencies. For
your part, don't be shy about Googling your prospects and
new clients, as well: The more you know about each other,
the more prepared you will be to determine whether the two
of you will be a good fit in an advisor/client relationship.

8. *Welcome questions.* It is a rare post-recession client who does
not qualify a financial advisor before making a commitment
to work with him or her, much in the same way the advisor
qualifies prospects before spending too much time wooing
them. New Web sites such as BrightScope Advisor Pages are
culling data from the Securities and Exchange Commission
and the Financial Industry Regulatory Authority to create

searchable online databases that tell "shoppers" about the work history and credentials of financial planners, brokers, and investment advisors. Potential clients are likely to ask about your average account size and about whether you give small investors the same attention as wealthy clients. They'll want to know your fees, how they can contact you, and whether you will return calls promptly. And they're likely to hold you to the commitments you make during this initial conversation—an indication of whether you are highly accountable and make good on your promises.

9. *Be transparent about your process, your track record, and your professional affiliations.* During the 1990s, when the price of stocks was doubling—or better—between monthly statements, few clients were concerned about how or why. Now that the numbers are more likely to slip than to soar, investors want to know everything from how much risk comes with an investment, to how your other clients' portfolios are performing, to your personal investment philosophy, to whether your firm retains custody of their assets or places them in the custody of an independent firm. In fact, even if they don't ask those questions, it's a good practice to weave those answers into every new-client meeting so your investors are clear about your ethical beliefs and about who has access to their money. Educate them about new regulatory safeguards and about how the standards in your own practice and parent organization protect investments, require you to give unbiased advice, and guard client privacy.

10. *Prepare to lose a few.* Whether you're just starting your career or you're a skilled and seasoned advisor, sales professional, or wealth manager, be brave enough to walk away from an unsuitable client. Even an investor whose faith in the financial services industry is shaky probably would not agree to meet an advisor if he or she were not hoping to connect

with someone trustworthy and accountable. So it's quite possible that the two of you will find some common ground and a comfort level that allows you to start a mutually profitable relationship. But every now and then, you'll run into a would-be client who will never trust any financial professional—and has decided, in fact, that absolutely none are trustworthy. If you have shared your values, revealed your processes, shown off your accomplishments, displayed your credentials, and offered references, there's nothing left to do but beg the prospect for his or her business. Don't do it. Know the kind of client you want to work with. Choose clients whose values align with yours. Work with those who embrace mutual respect, trust, and success. Know that they, too, are accountable for the success of their investments. Wish the others well, and show them the door.

You Are Accountable

Although *Where Winners Live* is chock-full of first-hand examples and step-by-step advisories from wildly successful investment experts, our book can't "make" you accountable. You already *are* accountable. We all are.

What a book, an inspiring story, or a successful role model *can* do is help you change your *mindset*.

Our hope is that the success stories, scenarios, tips, and recommendations in *Where Winners Live* will leave you with a mindset of 100 percent personal accountability. That mindset is available to everyone.

If, when you opened *Where Winners Live* for the first time, you had a mindset of 0 percent accountability, 100 percent is available to you. If you have lived with the mindset that you are accountable for only 50 percent of what happens in your life, 100 percent is available to you. If you started *Where Winners*

Live with the impressive mindset that you are accountable for 85 percent of your results and that circumstances beyond your control can take the credit (or blame) for just 15 percent, 100 percent is available to you.

Our hope is that *Where Winners Live* will elevate you to the highest, most consistent level of personal accountability that will create the successful life and career you want.

Personal accountability works. Be a winner. Let it work for you.

About the Authors

Dave Porter

Dave Porter is the managing partner of Boston-based Baystate Financial Services, the largest "hybrid" financial services agency (selling both investment and insurance products) in the United States. A one-time insurance salesman, Dave took over Baystate Financial at age thirty-five and has grown its revenues from $1 million to $100 million a year and its staff to nearly 300 financial planners.

Lauded for his accountable business practices by industry peers, the Boston media and his own associates, Dave is a Boston Business Journal Most Admired CEO, and Baystate has been on the publication's list of the Best Places to Work in Boston for multiple years. In addition, Baystate has been honored by the Greater Boston Chamber of Commerce as a Small Business of the Year and has been included on *Inc.* magazine's 500|5000 list of America's fastest-growing companies three years in a row.

Dave is a national speaker on building financial services organizations and is active in the Boston community. He is past chairman of the Young Presidents' Organization, sits on the Board of Trustees of Elon University, and serves as a board member of the Genesis Fund, Zoo New England and other Boston-area organizations.

Linda Galindo

Linda Galindo is president of Galindo Consulting Inc. in Park City, Utah, and has worked for more than 20 years as a consultant, keynote speaker, leadership development facilitator, and executive coach. The author of *The 85% Solution*, Linda has served as an executive coach for teams and individuals around the world and has particular expertise in the financial services and healthcare fields.

Linda is known as an "accountability thought leader" and is considered one of the country's most dynamic and knowledgeable organizational consultants. Her educational film, "Accountability That Works," with CRM Learning, is a bestseller worldwide. In addition, her workforce training program, The Accountability Experience, has enjoyed brisk sales since its release by Pfeiffer in December 2010. Her training material is CPE-certified, and *Where Winners Live* will be the mainstay of all educational offerings in the financial service sector.

Linda has received many awards for her speaking and business acumen. In 2002, the National Association of Women Business Owners-Utah Chapter named her the Woman Business Owner of the Year. She has served on the executive board of the United Way, Salt Lake City, as the chairwoman of board development. She is a faculty member for The Governance Institute, which specializes in healthcare governance, and for the Institute for Management. Linda also served for six years on the board of directors of the NASBA Center for the Public Trust (National Association of State Boards of Accountancy).

A one-time radio journalist, Linda spends a significant portion of her time as a keynote speaker, executive coach, and facilitator to executive teams.

Sharon O'Malley

Sharon O'Malley is a writer, editor, consultant, and educator. A journalist for more than 20 years, Sharon has worked as a newspaper reporter in the Washington, D.C., area, and as a reporter and editor for magazines and newsletters. Her articles have been published in *The Washington Times*, *American Demographics*, *Better Homes & Gardens*, the former *Working Woman* magazine and in dozens of newsletters and trade magazines.

Sharon worked on *The 85% Solution: How Personal Accountability Guarantees Success* (2009, by Linda Galindo) and has helped a number of authors and experts find their voice by helping them write books, columns, blogs and articles.

An adjunct faculty member with the University of Maryland's Philip Merrill College of Journalism and with University of Maryland University College, Sharon also coaches writers and conducts writing workshops for businesses.

Index